Roadmap
to Hell

Sex, Drugs and Guns
on the Mafia Coast

Barbie Latza Nadeau

ONEWORLD

A Oneworld Book

First published in Great Britain and Australia by Oneworld Publications, 2018
This mass market paperback edition published 2018

ISBN 978-1-78607-459-1 (paperback)
ISBN 978-1-78607-256-6 (eBook)

All photos, unless stated otherwise, courtesy of the Author

Typeset by Hewer Text UK Ltd, Edinburgh
Printed and bound in Great Britain by Clays Ltd, Elcograf S.p.A.

Oneworld Publications
10 Bloomsbury Street
London WC1B 3SR
England

Stay up to date with the latest books,
special offers, and exclusive content from
Oneworld with our newsletter

Sign up on our website
oneworld-publications.com

MIX
Paper from
responsible sources
FSC
www.fsc.org   FSC® C018072

In memory of all the nameless people who die with their dreams crossing the Mediterranean Sea every year.

For Nicholas and Matthew

CONTENTS

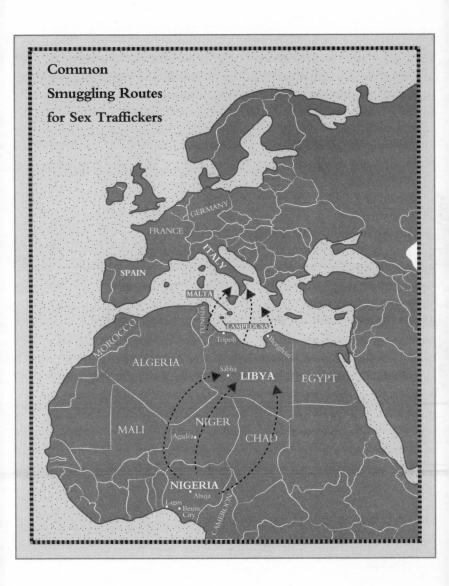

Common
Smuggling Routes
for Sex Traffickers

PREFACE

On 4 March 2018, Italians went to the polls in a gripping national election. The last election in 2013 had delivered a hung parliament in the Senate, where most of the work is done on legislation. As a result, the country filed through prime ministers at a rate of one every eighteen months. During that period, more than 600,000 migrants crossed the Mediterranean Sea into Italy. The 2018 elections made it further apparent that Italian opinion on their country was divided. The highest number of votes went to the maverick Five Star Movement, a pseudo party launched by comedian Beppe Grillo, a man previously known for bringing people to the squares to rail against the establishment. The second-highest percentage of votes went to Matteo Salvini's far-right League party, formerly a separatist party called the Northern League. The party's candidates have campaigned on anti-immigrant and xenophobic rhetoric since the 1990s. Since coming into power, the coalition have bulldozed Roma camps, banned the building of mosques and called for mass deportations of migrants arriving by sea.

After three months of wrangling, the League and Five Star formed an unlikely alliance and produced their lengthy "contract for a government of change" that melded their often divergent policies to create Italy's first populist government. They were given the mandate to govern and sworn in on 1 June, the day before Italy celebrates its Republic with parades and military flyovers.

The parties appointed Giuseppe Conte, an unknown law

professor with Five Star sympathies, to do the party leaders' bidding. Salvini took the Interior Ministry portfolio and is a deputy prime minister along with the Five Star's Luigi Di Maio, who heads the Labor Ministry in his first-ever paid job beyond being a waiter when he was younger. He lived at home with his mother until just before the election.

Salvini spent his first day in office in Sicily, where he visited a migrant and refugee camp in the southern port town of Pozzallo. There he lamented that Sicily had become "Europe's refugee camp." He was met with protesters calling him a fascist and telling him to go home. Still, he announced that it was the migrants who needed to "pack their bags" because, as he put it, "the party is over."

Anyone who has followed the migrant crisis in Italy, even on the most superficial level, would likely concur that there is no party for those who risk their lives to get to Europe. Instead, they often live in overcrowded and inhumane conditions or are forced into sexual slavery, as this book chronicles.

Salvini made a special shout-out to those "living in hotels" to get ready to be expelled. He vowed to turn reception centers into locked detention and expulsion centers, which is in direct defiance of European human rights laws which state that asylum seekers have a right to request protection. He said there would be a locked detention center in each province so migrants wouldn't be seen milling about where Italians shopped and did business. He said he wanted to clean up Italy and get migrants out of sight. "We need mass purification, street by street," he said in June.

While he was in Sicily, a rickety migrant boat sank off the shores of Tunisia killing more than 100 people. His response was to say that most of the Tunisian migrants were "criminals" and "felons."

A week into his government, Salvini kept another campaign promise by closing all of Italy's ports to non-Italian flagged NGO rescue boats, making political pawns out of the 639 people who had been rescued by the *Aquarius* ship run by Doctors Without Borders and S.O.S. Méditerranée. The ship, escorted by Italian naval and Coast Guard vessels, made a three-day crossing to Valencia in Spain, where the migrants and refugees were accepted.

Only Italian flagged vessels were allowed to deliver rescued people onto Italian shores. The *Aquarius* was soon back out at sea, but by early July they, along with all of the other NGO rescue ships, had ceased operations. Now, even migrants rescued by the Italian Coast Guard are held in limbo and only allowed to disembark if other European nations pledge to take some of them. Meanwhile, Libyan authorities have been given new boats by Italians in order to turn those departing their shores back to what most of the world has described as inhumane conditions.

Since the fall of 2017, all but three such organizations have suspended rescue operations because of increasing confrontations with the Libyan Coast Guard and increased pressure by Sicilian authorities. In August 2017, the rescue boat operated by the German NGO Jugend Rettet was seized on the island of Lampedusa for aiding and abetting illegal migration and has yet to be released. In March 2018, a rescue boat operated by the Spanish NGO Proactiva Open Arms was also sequestered for more than a month while a court battle ensued. The boat was finally released and is one of only three remaining NGOs conducting rescues at sea.

The new Italian government's promise to clamp down on migrants will not stop sex trafficking. It will only slow it down, forcing the traffickers to find other ways to get their precious cargo to Italy. New routes are already opening up that take the girls through Libya more quickly. In November 2017 several boats carrying hundreds of migrants sank off the Libyan coast. The bodies of twenty-six presumably Nigerian girls and young women were recovered. A mass funeral was held for them in Salerno where matching coffins lined the central square of the city's main cemetery. Only two of the young women had been identified. The rest were buried with photos of their faces, dental records and a number in cemeteries across Sicily. But what was truly remarkable about this tragedy was the fact that some of the girls had somehow escaped the horror of Libyan detention centers en route to Europe. The coroner told me that five of the girls had newly coiffed hair, manicures and clean clothes. The rest showed the tell-tale signs of abuse, some had been beaten and burned, most had parasites and scabies and two were pregnant. But it remained curious that some of the girls had been brought through on a faster route. They all ended up in the same boat, but there was a notable difference in the condition of the girls, which suggests new routes for trafficking opening up to get the girls to Europe more quickly. In late June, reports that young women were being shuttled to Italy by fast boat via the island of Sardinia further substantiated the theory that traffickers will continue to bring women in, no matter what.

Migration continues to be hot-button issue in Italy. Boats filled with desperate people continue to attempt to cross the sea. With the new government vowing to keep rescue boats from reaching Italy and quickly sending them back if they do, the situation seems sure to quickly escalate to a full-blown humanitarian crisis.

INTRODUCTION:
SETTING THE COMPASS

When I moved to Italy with my husband in February 1996, I admittedly knew nothing about this country. We were newly married and had left South Dakota in the American Midwest on a blustering snowy day with wind-chill temperatures hovering around forty degrees Celsius below zero. The sight of the green rolling hills and deep blue sea below our TWA 747 as we landed at Rome's Fiumicino Airport was nothing short of magical. The taxi driver even whistled "Smoke Gets in Your Eyes" as he drove us through the cobbled streets of the ancient eternal city with which I would soon fall in love. Twenty years, two sons and one less husband later, this country still captivates my soul. It delights me and infuriates me, but mostly it still challenges me to reconsider everything I assume to know. Nothing can be taken for granted in a place with such a complex past, and the rules I was used to in America have never applied here.

Not long after we arrived, I landed a dream job with *Newsweek* magazine, which gave me a front-row seat to the events that were unfolding around me. The European Union was just launching its single currency and Italy was modernizing in ways both good and bad to try to keep up. When I first arrived, everything was closed on Sundays and you could scarcely buy milk and flour in the same store thanks to protectionist laws that kept small businesses alive. Now the quaint, family-run businesses have largely disappeared, giving way to Chinese discount shops and twenty-four-hour grocers. Italy was a true monoculture back then; most of the foreigners were tourists or white expats like me. That has changed, too, with the influx of migrants and refugees coming into the country by sea; more than 181,000 mostly Africans arrived in 2016 alone, creating what is referred to simply as "the migrant crisis," even though many of the people coming over are also refugees in the truest sense of the word, fleeing war and persecution.[1] Few will ever be allowed truly to integrate into this society; they are rarely allowed to work behind the counters in the shops; instead, they seem destined to stand in front of them begging for loose change.

I have covered all sorts of stories during my time here, from lavish papal coronations to mass-casualty earthquakes. I've lost count of how many governments have fallen and how many leaders have been forced out of office in shame. There have been murder trials and cruise-ship wrecks and gala parties inside ancient monuments, but the most common storyline that I have covered is one that seems to be the subtle thread running through every major event in this country: Italy's endemic corruption.

It would be easy to blame this malady entirely on the country's major organized crime syndicates – such as the Sicilian Cosa Nostra, the Neapolitan Camorra or the 'Ndrangheta of Calabria – but it extends far beyond the mob. I have seen corruption in local and national government institutions and public schools, in the Catholic Church through the widespread cover-ups of clerical sex abuse crimes, and on my street when a traffic officer takes a bribe and tears up a ticket. But lately it is most apparent in the mishandling of the migrant crisis through the blatant exploitation and blind eye turned to what's happening to some of the most vulnerable people on earth.

When I think back to the first time I saw Italy from above, that wonderful day I moved here more than two decades ago, I wish I had understood how complicated the country below me really was. Understanding Italy's geographical location on the map is the key to deciphering its many challenges. The country, though one of the founding cornerstones of Europe, is as close to North Africa and the Middle East as it is to countries like Germany. South across the Mediterranean Sea from Rome is Sicily, whose western islands of Lampedusa and Linosa could have easily been a territory of North Africa, just seventy miles from Tunisia and a few hundred from Libya. It's little wonder the United States and NATO keep their strategic drone command center and Middle East and Africa surveillance hubs at the Sigonella base on the island. To the east, on the other side of Italy's boot, are the Balkans, Greece and Turkey, all just a ferry ride away.

When I first moved to Italy, several people told me that "Africa begins in Rome," which was something I didn't understand at the time, but certainly do now. The type of poverty that permeates much of Africa exists in parts of the Italian south as well. Almost two million Italian children live below the poverty line in the regions that start just a few kilometers south of the capital. UNICEF, the United Nations Children's Fund, says Italy has the highest overall percentage of people living in extreme poverty anywhere in Europe, primarily due to the mismanagement of resources and funds intended for its own people.[2] With that in mind, it's little surprise that leaders pay even less attention to vulnerable strangers.

Italy's major problems lie in its southern regions, known as the Mezzogiorno (literally "midday"), which holds a third of the country's population and all its organized crime hubs. Unemployment is highest here, hovering around forty percent in some areas, and so is the murder rate, which regularly tops ten murders a month in Naples, a city of just three million people. Puglia, the heel of Italy's boot, was the central entrance point for counterfeit cigarette and arms trafficking in the 1990s, during the height of the Balkan conflicts just a few miles across the Adriatic Sea. Basilicata and Calabria, which make up the boot's insole, still have villages without internet or schools.

Moving north towards Rome through Campania, from the toe of the boot, the Amalfi Coast is the sparkling diamond among a region that is easily the most lawless and dangerous in the country, made famous by Roberto Saviano's tales of death and despair in his bestselling book *Gomorrah*, all just a few hours' drive from Rome.

This southern Italy is not the stuff of guidebooks and post-cards. Its ports, as beautiful as they may be over a cocktail at sunset, hide unparalleled criminal activity as everything from deadly arms to stolen antiquities find their way past the often-corrupted customs officials.[3]

Lately, however, Italy's southern ports have become the gateway for a very different type of cargo, with hundreds of thousands of migrants and refugees arriving each year. I started covering the migrant crisis in 2009, when the blue wooden fishing boats bought from scrap yards by enterprising smugglers started washing up on the shores of Lampedusa, filled with economic migrants and those fleeing famine and dirty wars in Africa.[4] In the beginning, the smugglers would even navigate the old fishing boats themselves and then either escape on smaller speed boats that trailed them or wait until they got caught and were deported back to Tunisia or Morocco and do it all over again. Some of those old blue boats can still be seen, washed up on Lampedusa's coastline, but most have been hauled to the center of the island where they are piled high in what amounts to a gigantic boat cemetery.

It must be noted that the migrant crisis that impacts Italy is a very different one from that involving Syrian refugees in the rest of Europe. Italy's crisis started as a trickle of people coming from across the sea in North Africa to the Sicilian island of Lampedusa more than three decades ago. Arrival numbers rarely topped a few thousand a year. It picked up speed in the years before the Arab Spring, when mostly young men started arriving, but the uprisings that began in late 2010 marked a great change in number of arrivals, which suddenly started topping fifty thousand or more. This also led to a rise in human smugglers, who soon understood that the more desperate people were, the more they would pay for passage across the sea. When the Arab Spring exodus calmed down, the smugglers weren't ready to give up their profits and soon started actively searching out sub-Saharan African economic migrants and refugees fleeing war and persecution who wanted to take a chance on a better life in Europe, which seemed like a magical land of hopes and dreams until they realized that the opportunities weren't meant for them. It didn't take long for sex traffickers to realize they could use the established smuggling routes to ferry exploited women to Italy.

Of the women making the journey, I met so many who had both emotional and physical scars, with personal stories of war and torture, of mind-numbing poverty and death. Those stories that filled my notebooks have haunted me for all these years as I searched for a way to do them justice and find an audience who might be interested to know more.

Then, around 2012, something changed. The boats were increasingly filled with Nigerian women and, a short time later, so were the streets and back roads of Italy. Prostitution is legal in Italy, so sex workers from all over, including Nigerians and other sub-Saharan Africans, have always been part of the local landscape. But I noticed that the women who started showing up on the streets after 2012 were young and clearly scared. They were different – not the experienced sex workers who knew if a client was safe or not just by looking, but children the same age as my own, reluctantly getting into cars with men.

What bothered me most was not just that they had crossed the dangerous sea on a dream of a better life only to become sex slaves, but that everyone knew about it. Yet, for all the transparency in this tragedy, I soon discovered that only a few elderly Catholic nuns seemed to be trying to do anything to stop it.

Instead of helping these women, the focus on the migration crisis rests squarely on who should rescue the people on the smugglers' boats and where they should be taken. Millions have been spent by the EU on a program called "Sophia" to destroy smugglers' ships by lighting them on fire at sea once the people have been rescued, which has only resulted in smugglers using cheaper and far more dangerous rubber dinghies instead. The priority is never about who is on those ships and why, apart from the persistent fear that they might be Islamic State terrorists.

But consider this: in 2016, eleven thousand Nigerian women and girls arrived in Italy on those boats. More than eighty percent, that's around nine thousand, were trafficked specifically for sexual slavery in Italy and beyond, according to the International Organization for Migration (IOM), who say many of the rest are also lured into the sex racket upon arrival. When the figures are tallied for 2017, the number is likely to be the same or higher. It seems unthinkable to me that this phenomenon has been allowed to grow steadily for the last five years. I cannot help but wonder: since we know about it, why can't we as a society do anything to save these women?

Some argue that enough is being done just by saving them from drowning in the sea. Indeed, hundreds if not thousands of women who were destined for sexual slavery have drowned over the years when their boats sank. But saving women from death isn't enough if their destiny is a fate some would consider worse: sexual slavery.

When the smugglers' boats first started coming to Italy, the authorities did not allow rescues at sea as they eventually did with the advent of NGO search-and-rescue missions. Instead, the smugglers' ships had to crash quite literally onto the sharp rocks of Lampedusa, which is the closest chunk of land off the North African coast, before they could be rescued. The Coast Guard would use planes to monitor when the boats were coming in, but no one went out to rescue them, no matter how urgent their plight or how rickety the boats might have been. Aid agencies, such as UNHCR and Save the Children, that were set up in Lampedusa would then relay the information to journalists covering the crisis in an attempt to bring exposure to what was happening. Those of us who could convince our editors that the stories were worthy would fly to Lampedusa, an island so small you can see water on both sides of the landing strip as the plane touches down.

More than once I sat on the shores of Lampedusa after nightfall with other journalists waiting for a smuggler ship to crash, listening to the staccato blasts of the waves until the voices wafted ashore. They came in at night because of the lighthouse on the island, which led the way. The eerie noise preceded the outline of the boats, which looked like ghost ships caught between the moonlight and the passing lighthouse beams.

During one particularly horrific crash that happened right under Lampedusa's door-shaped memorial monument called the "Gateway to Europe," which had been erected in 2008 for all the mariners and migrants who had died at sea, there were splashing sounds tied to screams as people jumped off the boat. It was different from other wrecks because the boat was an enormous fishing trawler with a high mast and an actual navigational deck, rather than the smaller boats with telephone-box wheel rooms more common on fishing boats used for people smuggling. The wrenching sound of wood breaking seemed endless, as if the ship wouldn't stop crashing into the rocks.

Lights from the Coast Guard lit up the wreckage, its hull ripped open and a sea of humanity pouring out. I will never forget all those faces of the survivors as they scrambled towards us. It was not the time to conduct interviews. We put down our pens and cameras and helped them, carrying the small children and holding on to the pregnant women as they tore their bare feet open on the sharp rocks.

On that particular shipwreck assignment, which ended on the cover of the 20 June 2011 issue of *Newsweek* magazine, I met Dolly, a tall Nigerian woman with long braids of hair she had tied together with leather strings. We kept in touch for the next two years as she made her way to Sicily and eventually to the Italian mainland. I lost track of her after she left a refugee center near Florence, when her final asylum request was denied. A volunteer there confided that she was denied asylum because she had "run away to be a prostitute" somewhere in northern Italy. When I met her, she knew she might have to sell her body to survive "at first" but she had a real dream. She said she intended to open her own little shop in Venice one day, selling African handicrafts she would import from Nigeria.

In early 2017, I managed to contact Dolly after pleading with workers at the refugee center, explaining that I wanted to find out what had happened to her. After we got back in touch, she sent me a message and told me she had found work as a "window girl" in Amsterdam. She was paid fair wages and lived in a nice apartment by herself.

"It is not so bad," she wrote. "The men are clean and we get free doctor checks all the time."

She later updated me with news that she was planning to marry a Dutch man and quit sex work. The next time I tried to contact her, the email bounced.

Dolly is just one tiny piece of the long, sordid history of sex trafficking to Italy, one story out of thousands of women who came to Italy under different circumstances and who ended up selling their bodies by choice or by force. Whether Dolly chose to be a prostitute or was coerced into it is hard to know. She came at a time of transition, when most Nigerian women came to Italy with dreams that often worked out. That is no longer the case. Now that the sex traffickers piggyback on the migrant crisis, many of the exploited women end up in Italy whether they ever dreamt of coming or not.

It is a deadly and dangerous journey, and many of the trafficked women perish along with the thousands of migrants and refugees who die each year. But it seems that no one pays much attention to the deaths of those who aren't registered on passenger lists or whose families aren't waiting on shore. There is a hierarchy when it comes to tragedies, and the desperate have always been at the bottom. Reports of wooden boats or rubber dinghies going down with a hundred or even two hundred people barely make the news cycle.

In 2012, the *Costa Concordia* cruise ship, a giant ocean liner with more than 4,200 people on board, crashed onto the shores of the Tuscan island of Giglio. It was a spectacle made for TV. I spent weeks on Giglio, returning time and again over the next several years, even though 'just' thirty-two people had died. I have never been dispatched so often or for so long on a migrant story, where the death tolls were sometimes thought to be three times higher or more. Migrant shipwrecks are so common and the circumstances so vague that they all blend together, made worse by the fact that there are rarely any details about the people who have lost their lives. Unlike the *Costa Concordia*, where we had names, ages and nationalities, the migrants are nameless and faceless and often die without their family members even knowing. Whole smugglers' ships just disappear off the horizon. Sometimes rescuers find empty dinghies floating at sea or old blue fishing boats with a few dead people onboard. We will never know how many people were on those boats. They're just gone.

Several months after the *Costa Concordia* went down, a pair of migrant boats sank close to the shore of Lampedusa that did make the news. More than 360 migrants and refugees died, including a woman with her newborn baby still attached by the umbilical cord. The dead were retrieved from one of the sunken ships and eulogized at a mass funeral inside a hangar at Lampedusa's airport. Those incidents changed Italy's approach to migration. In 2013, it launched the Mare Nostrum program, spending €9 million a month on rescue missions to ensure there would be no more sinkings of that magnitude. However, only a year into the mission, under pressure from the rest of Europe to stop what was largely perceived as a program that encouraged illegal migration by creating a pull factor, and along with tight budget demands following a recession, the program was scrapped. The decision proved lethal and the death toll rose tenfold. The gravity of the danger became clear again when another ship went down in April 2015, with as many as nine hundred people on board.

By this time, NGOs were already taking matters into their own hands. The first was the Mobile Offshore Aid Station, or MOAS, launched by wealthy American entrepreneur Christopher Catrambone and his Italian wife Regina. During the summer of 2013, the couple and their family were sunning themselves on their yacht off the coast of Malta when an abandoned jacket floated by. Regina asked the skipper about it and when he explained that it surely belonged to a dead migrant, the couple decided to act. A million dollars of their own money and a year later, they were out saving lives. By the summer of 2017, there were more than a dozen charity ships run by well-known groups like Doctors Without Borders, Save The Children and S.O.S. Mediterranée, along with several run by smaller German and Spanish groups. The NGOs coordinate with the Italian Coast Guard, dispatching whichever ships happen to be closest to the smugglers' boats when distress calls are sent out and determining which Italian ports will receive those rescued.

The EU's border control agency Frontex has its own boats at sea as well, but they loathe the NGOs' work, publicly accusing them of creating a pull factor that they say invites more migrants to come, a criticism that was also leveled at the Mare Nostrum program back in 2013. It is unclear if that's true. There is no way to measure this. Of all the rescued migrants I've interviewed, not one even knew what an NGO rescue boat was. They were just thankful someone had saved them. What *is* clear, is that without the NGOs, the death toll would be more absurd than it already is. Even with a dozen NGO ships at sea, more than five thousand people died making the crossing in 2016, and Amnesty International says the death toll is getting worse, having increased threefold between 2015 and 2017.[5]

In the end, the fate of these trafficked women is the same, whether their boat crashes onto the island of Lampedusa or a charity ship picks them up. No matter what their circumstances are, almost all have endured the same horrific conditions and physical and mental abuse along the way. Many witness death along the desert trail and are kept in prison-like conditions in Libya, run by the militias that operate freely in the country while they wait for smugglers' boats to become available. Some women are given birth control by their traffickers so they don't end up pregnant as a result of the inevitable rapes along the way. When they are finally taken to the smugglers' boats, it is often at gunpoint. They are then pushed out to sea in boats that are not even remotely seaworthy. At that point, it doesn't really matter if it is a charity ship, a Frontex vessel, the Italian Coast Guard or a merchant ship that picks them up – they are just lucky to be alive.

Of all the nationalities making the treacherous journey, it is the rapid increase in Nigerians that has troubled authorities the most. Incremental increases in asylum requests from people from Syria, Eritrea or Somalia can be justified over the years by conflicts in those regions. Nigeria, on the other hand, is the richest country in Africa based on its GDP, of more than $405 billion, the twenty-sixth highest in the world, according to the world bank.[6] Despite having widespread corruption and extremes in poverty and wealth that impact the majority of its population, it does not fit the usual economic profile of a country from which asylum seekers should flee, which is reflected in the fact that few Nigerians are granted political asylum when they reach Europe.

Everyone who reaches Italy by sea has a right to apply for asylum, a process that can take more than a year, during which time they are mostly free to come and go from the state-run centers for asylum seekers. So even those who have no real chance at winning the legal right to stay can easily disappear into the country's vast undocumented population while they wait. Sex traffickers take advantage of that and many women destined for sexual slavery are never seen again after they apply for asylum. It shouldn't be this way. Nigeria has the economic power to help its people.

Yet Nigerian women are the single largest group of victims trafficked to Europe for the forced sex slave trade in a racket everyone knows about but no one stops. The US State Department says the government in Nigeria does not even comply with the minimum standards for the elimination of trafficking.[7]

Because prostitution is legal in Italy, there is an assumption that women selling sex on the streets are there by choice. Prostitution is often described as the "oldest profession in the world." But trafficked women do not make choices. Sexual slavery and sex trafficking are assault and systematic rape dressed up as prostitution. A woman who has been sex trafficked may stand on a street in skimpy clothing and solicit sex; she may smile and pretend she wants a client to pull over to the curb. She may willingly take him to a house and open the door to a bedroom. She may touch him, please him and satisfy his sexual wants. She may lie with him after. She may eventually even take what becomes a form of comfort in the familiarity of a regular client. But a woman who has been trafficked for sex is never doing these things by choice. She is threatened by an unseen captor she knows is watching her, whose punishment will be worse than the hand job or blow job or degrading sex act she has to endure. Punishment for not soliciting sex for Nigerian women who have been trafficked is, without exception, a fierce beating – the first time. After that, it is almost always brutal, violent gang rape or death.

What is almost worse than the fact that this skin trade exists in the first place is that this is not in any way a secret in Italy. Every nun, police officer, priest, prosecutor and aid worker who deals with the girls knows exactly how the corrupted system works, yet for some unthinkable reason no one has ever had the means, or maybe the will, to stop it. Despite everything I love about this country, its people and rich culture, this is one thing I can't ignore.

Dolly, a sex-trafficked woman, arrived in
Lampedus on board this migrant boat.

1

RESCUED, THEN CAPTURED

"If you don't call this number when you get to Italy, you will break the spell and your family will be killed." – Nigerian maman to sex trafficking victim

MINEO – Joy is a petite Nigerian woman who said she was eighteen when I met her in late summer 2016. She was waiting outside the CARA Mineo reception center for asylum seekers, one of the biggest refugee and migrant ghettos in Europe, for someone she didn't yet know to pick her up.[8] She looked much younger, wearing a faded denim jacket over a crisp white T-shirt and jeans that hugged her small figure. Six or seven strings of colorful beads were wrapped around her neck. A pretty gold chain hung from her left wrist. She smelled of talcum powder and mint chewing gum. She had left Nigeria six months earlier with the plan to come to Italy to work as a hair braider. She had been told that there was much work in African salons thanks to all the wealthy Nigerian women who had found success here. Italian beauticians simply didn't know how to style African women's hair, she explained.

Joy said she grew up in a poor family in a small village in Edo State with no electricity or running water. She was the oldest of six children and her parents were hard workers, but illiterate. When she was fifteen, she moved to Benin City under circumstances she can't clearly recall but, in retrospect, she suspects that her parents may have sold her in some way to raise money for their younger children. Her mother gave her the thin gold bracelet on her wrist to sell if she was ever desperate for money.

"They probably had no choice," she said as she looked down the road toward the thick citrus groves that hide the coming traffic. She had the wisdom that comes from being forced to accept a certain set of bad circumstances, but also the dangerous naivety of someone who had no idea what she was getting into.

As we spoke, a dark car came into view and she took a couple of steps away from me to make sure whoever was driving saw her, and saw that she was alone. There were a handful of other migrants loitering along the road, perhaps waiting for someone to pick them up or just passing the time they were allowed outside the barbed-wire fences. The approaching car didn't slow down, so Joy came back over to me and picked up the story about her parents.

"They had so many children and no money to feed them and I was old enough and smart enough to go to the city to work," she explained. "It was the best thing that happened to me – to get out of the village. I would still be there if I hadn't been sent away."

She ended up working as what one can only describe as an indentured servant for a wealthy Nigerian woman who owned a beauty salon in Benin City. She was told that her wages were sent to her parents in the village, though she has no idea if they ever received them because her parents didn't have a phone or internet and she had never gone back. There were six other girls who worked for the woman, whom Joy says they called their "maman," the French word for mother. It's a term often used to describe recruiters who find women in Nigeria for the Nigerian madams, or pimps, working in Europe. During the evenings, one of the women taught Joy how to read and write in fancy cursive, which she showed me by writing her name in my notebook.

When Joy first arrived in Benin City, she told me she had to wash floors and clean the bathrooms, but she eventually learned how to braid hair, which she often did for more than eight hours a day at the maman's salon.

When she turned sixteen, she took a JuJu curse that she remembers as terrifying. JuJu is a spellbinding curse that plays on faith, superstition and lack of education. It dates back to ancient African rituals performed in Edo State, where nearly ninety percent of trafficked women are from. It plays on a combination of Islamic, Christian and animist beliefs. Many women who have taken the curse but who then wish to escape its bonds sleep with a Bible or Qur'an under their pillow out of fear that they will die from the spell in their sleep.

The curse ties these Nigerian women to debt bondage that can only be paid back through forced sex slavery. "They took my period blood and mixed it with my toenails and some powders," she remembers, describing how the man also cut a tiny bit of skin from her breast near her nipple that she says left a small scar. "There was a lizard and a chicken, and a tiny dead animal like a baby mouse we had to swallow without chewing. There was also a loud drum. The smell was of spoiled meat. All the city girls who work for maman must do the ritual."

Her eyes were wide as she recalled the details of the story. The "priest" who performed the ceremony wore a red and white mask and had thick white scars on his chest and around his arms that Joy remembers staring at as she sat, semi-naked, in front of a small stone fire pit. They were inside a tent in a small grove of trees on the outskirts of Benin City. The priest then took all the elements used in the ritual and put them in a package along with the little bloody piece of skin and told her that if she broke the bond to her maman, her family in the village would die, and that she must do whatever her maman says to keep them safe. She was told that she must also promise to repay the maman for all the money she had spent on her. Joy agreed. She had no choice.

A few weeks after taking the curse, she was told that she would soon be moving to Italy, where she would work for her maman's sister.

At first, she said she was excited to go, but as the time to leave grew closer, she became anxious. She had no money of her own and knew no one at all in Italy. Still, she had no choice but to agree to the plan since her maman told her she had to do it, and she didn't want to break the curse. She had heard stories of girls going mad if they broke the curse, and she didn't want that to happen to her. She knew that as long as the witch doctor had the packet with her skin and toenails in it, he had control over her from Nigeria, and he would keep her safe as long as she followed the rules.

On the morning of her departure, her maman gave her fifteen thousand Nigerian naira, the equivalent of about €45, a cheap cellphone and an Italian phone number that she wrote in dark ink with a permanent marker on the inside of her left ankle, where her skin was lightest. She also wrote the number on a piece of cloth and sewed it into her jacket sleeve under the arm, below which she stored the gold bracelet from her mother in a seam. She had no passport or means of identification, no real possessions beyond a few changes of clothes, her hair braiding combs and the cellphone, which had a removable SIM card she was told to swap for an Italian one that she would get from the "church people" when she arrived in Italy.

"Don't lose this number," her maman told her. "If you don't call this number when you get to Italy, you will break the spell and your family will be killed."

The 4,800-kilometer trail from Benin City to the coast of Libya takes several days of solid driving on bumpy, narrow roads. Joy says she was stuffed into the back of a small bus commandeered by two Libyan men who took turns driving through the days and nights. A car with two or three armed men followed behind them. Joy was with twenty or more other young women and a handful of men in their late teens. They were not allowed to talk during the dusty journey, and they were given very little food and only warm water, which is a tactic used to avoid having to stop for bathroom breaks. But it was hot and the little water soon ran out. Towards the end of the journey, they became so dizzy and dehydrated that they had no choice but to drink their own urine, which they did by cupping it in their hands as they peed under blankets to keep the sand out.

Along the way, Joy remembers passing groups of men and women wrapped in yards of flowing material to protect their faces from the sand as they made their way on foot through the Sahara Desert. The drivers didn't pick anyone up, even when people tried to wave them down. Joy also saw skeletons protruding from the sand, some near small rock memorials, others just tufts of material strung on bones like flags in the wind. She has no idea which route they took, whether through Algeria and Tunisia or through Libya, but she remembers the journey lasting many long days.

They didn't stop in any towns, but sometimes they stopped at night so the men could sleep or do repairs on the truck. She and the other passengers slept on the ground under the truck, guarded by an armed man from the vehicle that followed them as the drivers slept beside a fire.

When they arrived in Tripoli, maybe a week later, the young men in their group were taken away. Joy heard later that all the men who come to Tripoli from Nigeria are held in appalling conditions in Libyan detention centers until money arrives from their families. Joy says she never paid any money at all and she never really considered why no one asked her to. She simply trusted that her maman had taken care of those details for her.

Even as she stood outside CARA Mineo, a world away from her homeland, she clearly felt indebted to her maman, whom she described in glorious terms of praise for giving her this opportunity, despite the hardships she had endured along the way and the uncertain future ahead. She genuinely believed she would work as a braider.

Once in Libya, she and the other women were taken to a small safe house near the coast, which she says was already filled with other African women. Several of them were pregnant, but none of them had children or husbands with them. The accommodation was dismal and most of the women slept on thin blankets on a wooden floor, leaving the mattresses for the pregnant women. There was one bathroom and no shower or bathing facilities, so the women used a garden hose that hung on a hook on the outside of the house to wash with cold water.

They were given rice to eat, but, again, very little water to drink. The water from the hose outside was brown and they were afraid it might make them sick. Joy thinks they stayed there for almost a week with nothing to do but wonder what would happen next. Joy told me she was so bored and worried that she even thought about killing herself, but she didn't know how she would do it, and, more importantly, she worried that suicide would break the curse and bring bad luck to her family in the village.

Every day more women arrived, but they didn't dare ask questions or talk to each other too much. There were whispers that women who "talked too much" had been taken away and raped and beaten or even killed. Joy said she thought day and night about her family in the village in Nigeria and wanted nothing more than to go back. She didn't care about the lack of running water or electricity. Anything had to be better than where she was at that moment, feeling hungry and scared and alone.

One morning, the two Libyan women who ran the safe house woke them early to tell them that they would be sailing to Italy that night. They removed all the food and water from the house, telling them that it was better if they didn't eat or drink before they got on the boat. After dark, a man came to the house. Joy said he was waving a gun like a madman and yelling at them to get out of the house. They could only take the clothes they were wearing at that moment, but Joy was able grab her jacket with her gold chain sewn inside and the cellphone number she had to call when she arrived in Italy.

They walked through tall grass toward the shore, where they were forced at gunpoint to join a group of African men who were already waiting on a very flat rubber dinghy. No one had the option to turn back and those who cried were hit or pushed to the ground. They were told to take off their shoes and leave them on the shore, where a young boy collected them in a plastic bag and took them away, likely to sell on the streets. They were told to go to the half-inflated boat and find a spot. Some people chose to sit in the middle. Joy straddled the edge.

The men quickly inflated the rubber boat with a noisy air pump run by a generator. Then the dinghy was pushed into the water. Joy estimated there might have been a hundred people with her. One of the men on the boat sat at the back using a small outboard motor that was barely strong enough to push the overcrowded dinghy through the rough waters of the sea. Fuel sloshed around the bottom of the boat, which burned Joy's skin and soaked through her clothing. The boat sailed toward the open sea for several hours. Joy said she and the other women cried as they watched the Libyan shore disappear behind them. She had no idea how to swim. Any time someone on the boat moved, the whole raft would start to twist and bend. Several people vomited over the sides or right into the bottom of the boat. There was no way to use a toilet so people just urinated or defecated in their clothing wherever they were sitting.

As the sun came up, the engine ran out of fuel and the raft started to drift in large circles. It was hot but Joy was afraid to take off her jacket. She was sure they would overturn and sink to the bottom of the sea. The day was long but as darkness came again, they saw a large boat with a spotlight on the horizon. One of the men held up a lighter to try to get its attention. The other men sitting next to her yelled and waved their arms, which caused the dinghy to bend and take on water. Finally, the spotlight from the larger vessel caught a glimpse of the dinghy and homed in on them.

Joy can't recall all the details from the actual rescue, but she remembers that a smaller boat came out and gave them all life jackets and then took them off one by one and ferried them in small groups to the larger vessel, which was operated by the Italian Coast Guard. Joy had seen very few white men in her life and she says she found the Italians strange-looking. After everyone was off the dinghy, the Coast Guard officers set it on fire and let it drift, sending up a big plume of dark smoke.

Once they were on the Coast Guard ship, they were checked for burns and signs of torture. Several of the men were treated for injuries from their time in the Libyan detention centers. The pregnant women were taken to a separate area of the ship. One of the nurses told a story about how a baby was born on the same ship after the mother had gone into labor during the rescue. Some of the women whispered about how they were pregnant from rape along the route through the desert or in Libya.

Several of the women who had been vomiting were given intravenous drips to rehydrate them. They were offered apples and water and a choice between sweet biscuits or salty crackers. They all slept on the deck of the ship wrapped in matching blankets. The ship sailed for two days and finally reached the Sicilian port of Augusta in the city of Catania, near the Mount Etna volcano and the CARA Mineo camp.

When they got off the boat, an Italian military policeman in a thick bulletproof vest stood guard with a gun as another man patted them down. The officers took knives from some of the men and when people had documents in their pocket, they were pulled from the line and sent to a woman with a clipboard.

They were taken to a large tent lined with army cots and told to sit or lie down. An officer accompanied by another Italian policeman with a gun went around the tent and asked their names and where they were from. A woman handed out shoes and flip-flops or white counterfeit Adidas sneakers that had been confiscated from illegal African sellers in Rome and Milan, who also started their journeys in ports like Augusta after crossing the sea. Another woman handed out bruised yellow apples from a large metal tub. An officer used a black marker pen to write a number on their left hands. Joy was number 323. No one took fingerprints or pictures of them, but sometimes migrants do have to have their pictures taken, holding up their numbered hands by their faces. That usually happens when the migrants are rescued by NGOs like Doctors Without Borders or Save the Children. When the Italian Coast Guard does the rescue, there are officers onboard the ships with guns who often carry out the initial fingerprinting and documentation of those rescued at sea. When the charities do the rescuing, there are generally nurses with cookies and hot drinks.

Once they were patted down and numbered, Joy says they were divided up into groups and directed towards large buses that were parked outside the tent. Joy's bus was headed to CARA Mineo.

Just like her maman in Benin City had told her, a charity run by the Catholic Church gave Italian phone cards to all those who had been rescued, which they were told they could use to call home. Joy didn't have a phone number for her maman to call and let her know she had made it safely to Italy. The number on her ankle had faded away when her foot was in the fuel at the bottom of the rubber dinghy, but she still had her jacket with the phone number sewn inside.

She turned on her phone and, after inserting the Italian SIM card, dialed the number. The line was busy. She kept trying during the short bus ride to CARA Mineo. The woman who finally answered told her to apply for political asylum using a fake name and birth date, and never to give the phone number she had just called to anyone.

Joy applied for asylum the morning after she arrived using her own birthdate and the name of her younger sister. She figured that maybe, if the asylum request went through, her sister might be able to come over, too. She would teach her how to braid.

Once migrants apply for asylum, which is a general application that could result in anything from full legal residency and permission to travel around Europe to a much more common ninety-day permit to stay, they are free to come and go from the center at designated times as they wait for word about their application, which can take many months. After three days, a man inside CARA Mineo, whom Joy did not recognize, found her and told her she was to wait at the roundabout down the road from the Mineo camp every morning and eventually someone would come and pick her up. Joy asked how she would know who was picking her up. "You will know," the man told her. "Just get into the car when it stops."

Joy was put in a villa with ten other Nigerian women around her age. Many of them were also coming to Italy for jobs as braiders. Some were coming to be prostitutes, even though they said that they really didn't want to. They all had contact numbers to call. Joy was afraid to get too friendly in case one of them worked for a competing hair salon.

Migrants like Joy who have applied for asylum are given a few euros of pocket money, paid for by the Italian state, which gives each center a sum per asylum seeker. The reimbursement is meant to cover the expenses of running the facility, though many facilities spend far less, cutting corners on food and other amenities, and pocket the residual profits. Some asylum seekers save up the money for train fares or to pay smugglers for the next leg of their journeys. Joy used hers to buy a new braiding comb at the makeshift Suk bazaar inside the camp, since she had had to leave hers at the safe house in Libya, and she knew she would need one for her new job.

When I asked Joy what she thought would happen when the person she was waiting for picked her up, she said she was sure she would be taken to a beauty salon owned by her maman's sister, where she'd be given a job as a hair braider like she'd had in Benin City. She said she might have to start by cleaning floors like she did then, but that eventually she was sure she could work her way up because she was very precise with her work.

I asked her if she knew that a lot of girls like her ended up as sex workers. She said she had heard about the Nigerian women who end up as prostitutes when they came to Italy, and she said that she would "never do that" no matter how desperate she got. I left it at that, but later I would regret not trying to warn her in a more concrete way. At the time, however, she was just one of so many young women I saw sliding into the abyss.

Eventually, she had to go back inside the compound or she risked not getting back in time for her evening meal. Once again, her ride had not come. I wished her good luck and gave her my phone number, which she saved in her phone before walking through the sliding metal gate back into the center.

The CARA Mineo reception center, down the hill from the village of Mineo in central Sicily, is a hellish ghetto where the vast majority of African migrants who arrive by sea start their lengthy journey to either asylum or the criminal world. It is often so overcrowded that people have to sleep on the floor or outside in tents during the summer months.

The center is known locally as *Cara* Mineo, which is grimly ironic, given that CARA, which stands for Centri di Accoglienza per Richiedenti Asilo, or welcome center for asylum seekers, is also an Italian word (*cara*), meaning "beloved" or "dear" in English. The center fits neither description. Instead, it is overrun by cockroaches and rats that feed off the garbage that is left festering in piles. Mangy, flea-infested dogs duck in and out of holes in the razor-wire fence that runs along a pocked road leading to Mount Etna, Sicily's live volcano, with its steady stream of smoke clearly visible in the distance.

It is a punishing purgatory for migrants hoping to become

refugees. It is also a hotbed for illicit activity, effectively sponsored and paid for by the Italian state. Organized thugs working with the Sicilian mafia known as the Cosa Nostra, the 'Ndrangheta criminal network based in Calabria, and the Camorra based in Naples easily find recruits to work as drug mules and petty criminals among the bored and idle men who have given up hope for the life they dreamed of before they crossed the sea.

Islamic State sympathizers are among the desperate, too, hoping to recruit fighters and haters of the West. In March 2017, Catania's chief prosecutor Carmelo Zuccaro, who has campaigned against the legality of NGO charity ships rescuing migrants at sea and bringing them to Italian shores, gave *Il Giornale*, a right-wing newspaper owned by Italy's flamboyant former Prime Minister Silvio Berlusconi's brother, an interview. In it, he revealed that the state had started investigations into prisons and refugee camps where extremists were recruiting migrants awaiting word on their asylum procedures. "We have received very specific reports of recruitment activities and radicalization," he told the paper. "There are radicalized individuals who attract foreigners in order to incite them to fundamentalism."

The fear of radicalization is quickly overshadowing the fact that the center has also become a haven for its own internal traffickers, who, posing as asylum seekers, facilitate the transfer of Nigerian women to their madams who will act as their pimps.

The center's population is transient. Those from Syria, Eritrea and Somalia, who are often given asylum semi-automatically, rarely spend more than a night, if that, at the camp. Families and unaccompanied minors are moved out quickly, too, often housed in centers sponsored by the Catholic Church on the Italian mainland. Nigerians make up the bulk of the residents at the center, just as they comprise the largest demographic group of all irregular migrants arriving in Italy, followed by those from other sub-Saharan African nations, especially

Guinea and Ghana. Around half of the Nigerians in the center are Muslim and a little less than half are Christian, reflecting the demographic makeup of their home country.[9]

The rest of the CARA Mineo residents are Bangladeshi, Afghani and Pakistani single men who were working in Libya when the country fell into disarray, and who often languish for months, or even years, waiting for their asylum requests to be heard. Once they have applied for asylum, they are free to leave the center during scheduled rotations. They must sign in and out. If they don't come back to the center, generally after a five-day grace period, their asylum requests are pulled and they are quickly forgotten. There is no effort to find them and bring them back or deport them to their country of origin.

When asylum requests are rejected, as they often are, the applicant used to have the right to appeal the decision twice, which, if nothing else, bought them more time to make an alternative plan to stay and move north into Europe. In 2017, the Italian government changed the rule and applicants can only appeal a rejection once, after which they are given a slip of paper that says they have five days to leave the country, though they are given no means to do so. Torn up shreds of those papers are a common sight along the road ditches to and from the center.

The complex that houses CARA Mineo was built in 2005 by the Pizzarotti Company of Parma, which is still the primary contractor for American defense logistics in Italy. It was designed as luxury off-base family housing for American military officers stationed at the Sigonella Naval Air Station base about forty kilometers away. The Americans who lived there called it the "Village of Oranges," named after the Sicilian blood orange and citrus groves that line the provincial highway that winds its way through the flat plains near Catania.

The American-style boulevards and tree-lined streets of the compound were meant to replicate a sterile American suburb to make the military families feel more at home. And it was just that, complete with all the trappings of suburbia. In the center of the complex was a mini city, with a recreational center, super-market, American-style steakhouse and a local coffee and pastry shop. The complex had an office suite and an internet point. There was a baseball diamond and American football field, too, along with a non-denominational house of worship that was used for weekly services by Baptists, Catholics, Protestants and Lutherans and doubled as a cinema, where American movies were shown on a big screen in the evenings.

More than four hundred two-level ochre, yellow and single and duplex villas, most with three bedrooms and three bathrooms, were built to accommodate the standard family of five comfortably. Large sloped terracotta awnings gave way to manicured lawns with massive American-style barbecues. The whole setup looked ridiculously out of place in southern Italy.

The off-base housing was intended for around two thousand inhabitants, but it was never very popular, and most American military families chose to live in the similar Marinai housing complex, which was much closer to the Sigonella base.[10] In 2011, the US Navy gave up its $8.5 million annual lease and returned the expansive property to the Pizzarotti Company.[11]

The same year, Silvio Berlusconi's government decided to lease the complex as an asylum "hot spot" to process a growing number of Arab Spring asylum seekers who were coming to Italy in droves. At that time, the complex was completely locked down and the mostly Tunisian and Moroccan migrants were held until they were repatriated to their countries. Now the people inside are called "guests" and are free to come and go as long as they have applied for asylum.

Ghosts of the center's former life remain, but everything seems askew, as if a movie is being filmed against the wrong backdrop. The compound's football field and baseball diamond have been repurposed for soccer, the old goal posts and gravel infield awkwardly out of place. The playground equipment

scattered throughout the sprawling compound is rusty and in
disrepair, now primarily used by young men in their twenties
who sit in the swings and lie on the slides to pass the long
hours. The compound's bar is now the medical center, the
restaurant a canteen where migrants pick up rations of rice and
bananas. The recreation room is a makeshift school for illiterate
adults and young migrant children, and the office suite has
been turned into a housing dorm for nearly four thousand
people.

The entire compound is lined with tall razor-wire fences
that used to keep intruders out, but have now been turned to
keep migrants in. The inhabitants often hang their laundry to
dry alongside disparaging signs against the Italian government,
condemning the bad food and the time it takes to process
asylum requests. The center is guarded by armed military
police who check the asylum seekers in and out and keep out
anyone who isn't registered. The incentive to return each
night runs beyond the food and shelter. They come back for
the promise of documents that will allow free movement
through Europe's Schengen territories and give them monthly
stipends to rebuild their lives. Still, dozens of people disappear each month, quickly replaced by new arrivals fresh from
Sicily's ports.

During harvest seasons, many of the men leave CARA
Mineo during the first furlough rotation in the early morning
and gather along a triangle of bare dirt where State Highway
417 meets the provincial road. They wait for local farmers who
come with open-backed pick-up trucks looking for "i neri," the
blacks, choosing the biggest and strongest for temporary labor
harvesting tomatoes and citrus fruits. It is a scene that could
be straight out of a slave trade movie. The farmers call them
ragazzo or "boy," asking them to turn around or show them how
straight their backs are. It is a degrading display made worse
only by the fact that they are paid slave wages, a mere fraction
of what Italians would be paid for the same work. Their wages

are part of the illegal black-market economy that makes up around twenty percent of Italy's overall GDP.[12]

Those who don't want to work or leave the compound simply do nothing all day long until they are eventually lured into the underworld. The conditions are deplorable. Most of the villas house fifteen to twenty people, who sleep in bunk beds or on mattresses arranged on the floors throughout the houses, even in the rooms that were originally intended as the living-area units. The villas are falling apart and the migrants, many of whom are unfamiliar with European plumbing and electricity, are left to do what they can to take care of the maintenance with scant tools. Toilets are almost always blocked and the stench of sewage permeates the grounds, attracting rodents and insects. There is no cleaning service on the premises outside of the administrative and kitchen areas.

Some of the villas are burnt out. Others are missing windows and doors that have been replaced by sheets of plastic or faded blankets. The Pizzarotti Company removed all the air-conditioning units, washing machines, barbecues and most of the valuable amenities like ceiling fans and bathtubs when the Americans left, leaving raw wires and holes in the walls and ceilings. The migrants and refugees have to wash their clothes by hand and hang them to dry.

Most of the residents live divided up according to their ethnic or religious background, which fosters tension and infighting. There are many different communities, but no real sense of community. The camp's rules are strict and trouble-makers are sometimes shipped off to local jails and are rarely heard from again, although, for some reason, those working as on-site traffickers never seem to get caught unless they break other rules.

In December 2016, four Nigerian asylum seekers led by a twenty-five-year-old man named Godswift Chukuma were arrested in their run-down villa in CARA Mineo, accused of drugging and raping a female resident in what was a noted deviation from the normal types of criminal activity in the center.[13] The other men, Solomon Obuh, twenty-one, Michael Okova, twenty-five, and Fedricic Johnson, twenty-three, had threatened her with death, beating her with iron rods and promising to kill her if she went to the police, which she did anyway.

Francesco Verzera, a bespectacled prosecutor in the region of Caltagirone, which has jurisdiction over criminal cases inside CARA Mineo, used the incident to plead with the Italian government authorities to close down the lawless camp, stating that overcrowding and lack of supervision is creating a dangerous criminal environment. "This sort of advocated violence that goes unchecked will soon become the norm if you continue to operate a community-based asylum center with nearly four thousand people like you do now," he warned. "The crimes continue to get more violent and the growing disregard for life is a clear sign of a deteriorating situation."

What Verzera later discovered was that the woman, realizing she was being trafficked for sex when she, like Joy, was told to go out and wait on the street for someone to pick her up, had refused to leave the camp to join her madam. The men, presumably working for the madam as her henchmen, violently gang raped her as a warning, which is the sadistic tactic most often used in sex trafficking, especially when young women are not compliant. The theory is that if a woman realizes that the punishment for not prostituting herself is violent gang rape, she will likely agree that blow-jobs and roadside sex are a better alternative. It is rare to meet a trafficked woman who has not been faced with this choice.

The camp's director is Sebastiano Maccarrone, who cut his teeth heading the migrant reception center on Lampedusa, where most migrants arrived on rickety boats before active rescues became the norm. Maccarrone readily admitted in a series of interviews in early 2016 that it was virtually impossible to control the activity among the inhabitants. "It's like a small city. The big crimes get reported, but the smaller ones are usually handled among the residents," he said, insinuating that violent gang rape was a smaller crime.

A few months after he sat for an interview, he was put under criminal investigation for corruption, accused of using funds intended for the care of migrants and refugees for personal profit in a scandal that reverberated all the way to Rome, with the discovery of a mafia organization tied to the capital city's government. However, by the end of the year, he was back at the helm of the center.

Every single person at CARA Mineo is supposed to have applied for a right to stay in Europe, either refugee status, political asylum or humanitarian protection, in accordance with the 2003 Dublin Convention, which requires migrants to apply in the country in which they first enter the EU[14] Many make the application, collect a few weeks' worth of their spending money and then set out for northern countries where there are better opportunities for integration.

But crossing north into Europe isn't guaranteed. In 2011, photographer Alex Majoli and I followed a group of about a dozen Tunisian men to the town of Ventimiglia on the Italian–French border. Each night at midnight they got on the late train and tried to make the crossing. Each night they got kicked off and sent back to Italy on the train. One night I met a man with bleeding gums on the train heading back across the border. He showed me his front teeth that he had picked up off the ground when the French border guard hit him with a baton.

The EU member states are supposed to accept and resettle a certain number of asylum seekers and refugees each that come in through any of the union's border nations. The quotas vary depending on the country's population and the number of arrivals. Most of the wealthier EU nations protested and, in 2017, the European Court of Justice ruled that member nations do not, in fact, have an obligation to resettle refugees who do not come via legal asylum procedures, such as programs set up at refugee camps in Jordan and Lebanon.[15] The ruling was meant to dissuade people from taking the risky sea journey by sending a message that they are not welcome, though few migrants I have ever talked to followed inner EU politics. Instead, most assume they will be allowed to traverse Europe as they wish, either to join family or find a place to settle down.

Some migrants who wish to wait and apply for asylum in northern Europe where they have family and other connections that might help them secure a legal right to stay, or who are being advised by traffickers like Joy was, do go through the motions in Italy with false information, especially if they come from countries that do not meet the legal definition of a country where conditions are bad enough to be protected from, like Nigeria. Their fingerprints and details are entered into the EU's digital cross-referencing database known as EURODAC, which purports to track anyone who has applied for asylum in Europe, in order to avoid multiple asylum applications.[16] Its effectiveness relies on each country uploading its asylum seekers' prints and information, which has proven a logistical challenge, especially when thousands of migrants arrive at the same time, which is often the case in Sicily.[17] The EURODAC data is kept for ten years and is also used by law enforcement authorities like Europol.

UNHCR also keeps a database of migrants and refugees whom they assist called ProGres, which keeps track of health records and family ties for around seven million refugees worldwide. This database is far more extensive and they use the information to provide assistance to transient refugees. They refuse to share any of the information with border patrol authorities or police.

Anis Amri, the Tunisian ISIS sympathizer who slaughtered a dozen people with a stolen freight truck at a Christmas market in Berlin in 2016, is the perfect example of the failed system. Amri was on one of the many thousands of migrants who arrived in Lampedusa in 2011.

Shortly after arriving, he was convicted of arson for his role in setting the reception center on Lampedusa alight during a protest against the over-crowded conditions. Sometimes migrants fleeing violence in Tunisia and Morocco had to sleep in parking lots under sheets of plastic because the centers were overcrowded and authorities were wary of moving the men to the Italian mainland where they might escape. Flaring tempers led to many protests during those years and it was common for the army to be sent to the tiny island to help keep order.

Even though it was long before ISIS became a household term, Italy's right-wing leaders, led by the Northern League's Umberto Bossi, planted the seed that terrorists would be smuggled in among what was then mostly Tunisian and Moroccan men. In the case of Amri, they would eventually claim to be proven right, even though there is no evidence that he came over with the intention to kill. He was a troubled man, according to prison records and interviews with his family back in Tunisia, but they say he changed for the worse during his time in prison.

Italian authorities have concluded that he was radicalized in Palermo while serving a four-year sentence before going on to kill in the name of ISIS. Even though he is a rare example of the worst-case scenario, he is exactly the type of boat migrant Europeans continue to fear most.

Amri's request for political asylum in Italy was denied and, after his stint in prison, he was supposed to be deported back to Tunisia. But the Tunisian government wouldn't recognize him or give him travel documents and the Italians had no valid reason to keep him in jail once his sentence was served, so he was set free. He moved north to Germany through Europe's open border countries where he applied for asylum once more. Denied again, he carried out the Christmas market attacks and then traveled back south through France and eventually returned to Italy where he was shot during a routine document check at a train station near Milan by a novice police officer in December 2016.[18] Despite being a known ISIS sympathizer who had previously been expelled from Italy, he was easily able to re-enter the country undetected. He was also under surveillance in Germany for terrorist ties, but no one had found a reason to lock him up.

Even if EURODAC were fully functional, fingerprints aren't always processed efficiently at CARA Mineo, meaning the prints might never be cross-checked. After an initial interview with local police, the applicant's asylum paperwork is sent to Rome to process, and the backlog means it's around two years before an immigration officer even looks at an application. That's why it is so easy for young women who are trafficked to disappear.

Almost all the Nigerian women and girls rescued from the smugglers' boats by the charities or Coast Guard vessels are from the small villages around Benin City in the southwestern Edo State. Most are single and traveling alone. More than eighty percent are "sponsored" by sex traffickers who have paid for their journey, according to the International Organization on Migration (IOM). The rest will have paid the smugglers themselves, but will likely not escape the eventuality of the sex trafficking rings that search out and prey on these vulnerable women.

It is important to note that the vast majority of Nigerian women are not running away from Boko Haram, the Islamic extremist group that thrives in the northeastern regions of Nigeria and that famously kidnapped 276 school girls from Chibok in 2014. Instead, the women who come to Italy tend to fit a very specific profile: they are very young and very poor and often without formal education – a combination that makes them easy to exploit in Nigeria and to convince that there is work for them in Europe.

Educated women are trafficked as well, but they generally fly in on fake visas rather than come in on rickety boats, often falling for the same false promises of legitimate work. The horror stories of what happens to the women and girls once they get to Italy rarely make it back to Nigeria, often because the women are too embarrassed to admit what they are being

forced to do or they feel ashamed that they fell victim in the
first place. Some are rightly concerned that their families will
disown them if they speak out. Instead, they unwittingly help
perpetuate the trafficking cycle by lying about what they are
really doing in Europe. In 2016, more than eleven thousand
Nigerian women came to Italy – more than eighty percent are
known to be trafficked as sex slaves. The number for 2017 is
estimated to be the same or higher.

Many of the Nigerian women trafficked for sex slavery are
assured by their "sponsors" that they will "take care of getting
the documents for them" once they leave the reception centers
like CARA Mineo. Others are told to make up information or
are provided with detailed false information that they are asked
to use for their applications, given to them by those they call
when they get to Italy or the traffickers who pose as asylum
seekers and operate inside the centers who guide them through
the well-oiled process that skirts the law. In fact, the trafficked
women often do end up with documents, albeit only thanks to
the extensive false document network operated by Italy's various mafia organizations. The documents, which often pass the
smell test with local authorities, are another link in the chain
that keeps them tied to sexual slavery because the madams
threaten to take them away if they try to leave or
underperform.

Eurostat did a study of Nigerian asylum requests granted in
Italy in the first nine months of 2015. Of the 11,340 requests,
510 were given full refugee status and 720 were given limited
humanitarian protection, which is the category below full refugee status but allows a two-year permit to stay in the country.[19]
Most of those who were given protection were unaccompanied
minors or pregnant women or those who had realized that they
were being trafficked for sex work. Some women who were
systematically raped or tortured along the desert trail or in Libya
are also given a right to stay if their injuries are bad enough. In
a few rare cases, Nigerian men who can prove they or their

families have been threatened or killed by Boko Haram terrorists in Nigeria are also given a pass. Despite so few Nigerians being given legitimate documents, thousands of women forced into sexual slavery have false papers.

There is often ambivalence when it comes to processing requests by Nigerian women, in large part because even the officials assume to know why they are really there, no matter what they are told. Some migrants have been coached what to tell authorities that might give them the best chance at being granted asylum, even if it's not entirely true. Italian authorities processing the massive number of requests, which lately number more than 150,000 a year, have neither the time nor the resources to try to carry out background checks on everyone. When a Nigerian woman says she has been threatened in Nigeria, or that her family has suffered under the corrupt government, or that she worries about Boko Haram, the authorities can be reluctant to believe her stories and just choose to see a prostitute in the chair in front of them. In these cases, the authorities may even know she is being trafficked and forced to sell sex against her will, but they still look away. As well as being short on time, they simply don't have a mandate for that sort of social service.

Such is life in CARA Mineo and other camps like it, where a long list of priority cases comes before those trafficked for sex work, and where the longer people stay, the more corrupt they become.

Those who built CARA Mineo for the American military families likely had no idea what it would become, though it does operate like a small city, even if most of the amenities are provided clandestinely by the asylum seekers rather than the administration. There are little restaurants, barbers and even witch doctors who operate out of the center's villas, and guests can find almost anything they want at the African souk-style bazaar where handcrafts, tobacco and supplies smuggled into the center are sold and traded. Alcohol is forbidden, and so are drugs, but residents say even what's forbidden is available for a price.

Angela Lupo, a legal adviser for the Italian Council for Refugees (CIR) told a parliamentary committee in 2016 that the center runs the risk of complete lawlessness. "There's talk of prostitution, of drug trafficking, there is certainly a lively black market," she testified. "The residents sell clothes, food, cigarettes and phone cards at bazaars dotted around the center. There's even an illicit restaurant and a migrant-run taxi service. The controls are few and far between."

Women are coerced into selling sex inside the camp, too, but they are rarely Nigerian. Instead, those who run the sex trade clearly know that the Nigerian women have already been exploited, so they tend to prey on women from other African nations like the Ivory Coast or Ghana. Nigerians occupy the top rung of the hierarchy of criminal gangs operating within the center because they outnumber the other nationalities and, because of that, they are the ones who have forged ties with the local mafia and other organized crime syndicates in Italy, for whom they can easily provide drug runners and others who might eventually enter a life of crime, especially if their asylum request is denied.

Of CARA Mineo's average of four thousand residents, most are men. There are only around six hundred women at any given time. Sex is a currency at the camp, often traded for drugs, cigarettes or other supplies in lieu of cash.

In 2012, a Caltagirone prosecutor opened an investigation into forced prostitution inside the facility tied to a spate of abortions carried out by doctors treating patients from the center. In the first three months of that year, the center's doctors performed thirty-two abortions on migrants, which constituted an increase of more than two hundred percent from the year before. The abortions were not due to what are considered normal migrant factors, such as maternal health, which often results from malnourishment or from the dangerous sea voyage. Nor were the women requesting abortions claiming rape in Libyan camps before they set sail to Italy. Instead, authorities concluded that the high number of abortions was due to the increase in prostitution within the camp, coupled with the lack of birth control options. Because of extensive Catholic Church donations and influence over migrant and refugee care, contraception was not being distributed, and few migrants have the financial means or even access to stores to source their own. Since then, some aid groups are rumored to be handing out condoms to women suspected of being forced into selling sex inside the center.

The camp is uninviting after a long period of time and most people whose asylum requests are delayed simply leave because they can no longer tolerate the substandard quality of life. Those inside the camp are treated with something far less than human dignity. During the 2016 investigation into the seventeen camp administrators, prosecutors alleged that refugees were essentially bought and traded at the highest levels for kickbacks. A common complaint has long been that the meals are cheap and starch-based with no daily variety, generally rice and bread and heavily processed meats served with overripe bananas and apples that have been rejected by local growers. Children are given long-life UHT milk, but there are few vegetables on offer. Providing sub-standard food is a common ploy for centers to bilk the system of state-funded reimbursements that are supplemented by the EU. By offering bulk foods, like rice, that cost just pennies a plate, they can save money. That's why smaller refugee centers, where treatment is often more personalized, struggle to make ends meet. It becomes very difficult to provide for a person's total needs, even including the money that the government provides per migrant.

On average, around ten migrants waiting for their asylum requests to be heard die at CARA Mineo every year, often killed in fights or because they have medical conditions that aren't tended to, according to Amnesty International and other aid groups that work in the center. In 2016, a young man from

Ghana named Ebrahima Fati was killed by a local Sicilian woman driving her SUV too fast along the citrus grove-lined road that passes by the camp. His death sparked angry protests in the center when the woman wasn't charged with a crime, despite multiple witnesses – all migrants – testifying that she was driving at an excessive speed. Her defense was that she was afraid that the migrants might stop her car and hurt her.

In 2015, a thirty-one-year-old man from Pakistan was found dead behind the villa he shared with other Pakistani nationals. His death was ruled natural, despite his young age and lack of known medical problems. Autopsy results were incomplete and because he had no family to speak of, there was apparently no real reason to find out just how he died.

Suicide is common, too, especially for those whose asylum is denied, and sometimes for those who just can't wait any longer to hear the outcome. In 2013, a spate of more than a dozen suicides culminated with the death of a twenty-one-year-old Eritrean man named Mulue, who hung himself with a curtain from his room. The center administrators responded by removing the curtains in most of the villas.

The reality is that migrants are treated as second-class citizens in the eyes of the law and in public perception. This isn't unique to Italy or to African migrants. In 2016, Hungarian authorities were caught on videotape throwing loaves of bread over a tall fence to crowds of Syrian refugees as if they were dangerous animals.[20] Such attitudes play a role in the EU's inability to come up with a strategy for the ongoing crisis. Italy is especially schizophrenic on this, at once rescuing tens of thousands of migrants from the sea and at the same time treating them without the basic respect for human dignity once they have been saved. Even if they are granted asylum, things don't always improve. In August 2017, a group of around eight hundred mostly Eritrean and Ethiopians who had been granted political asylum were kicked out of an old office building in Rome they had been staying in illegally for around four years.

When those who had nowhere to go after the evictions camped out in a nearby park, police removed them with water cannons. These were people who had been granted full protection by the Italian state but who had not been provided with housing or income.

Sister Rita Giaretta runs Casa Ruth shelter for trafficked
women in Caserta. Photo courtesy of Sister Rita Giaretta.

2

NUNS IN THE LAND OF FIRE

"The only rule is that there are no rules." – Sergio Nazzaro, journalist

CASERTA – Sister Rita is driving too fast, but the last thing the cops are looking for is a speeding nun. The sixty-year-old Italian can barely see over the steering wheel of her white minivan as she barrels down the pocked highway that cuts across the patchwork of mostly overgrown farmland north of Naples. She is headed from Casa Ruth, the shelter she runs for trafficked women on the main street of Caserta, to the Via Domitiana, a twenty-mile stretch of road cut in half by a backwater town called Castel Volturno that has become a veritable boot camp for Nigerian women exploited for the forced sex trade that is endemic in this part of Italy.

Squalor is everywhere. Big bags of garbage that line the thoroughfare have been ripped open by the wild dogs that roam the area. A makeshift dump in one of the bus stop alcoves is stacked with sullied mattresses, broken kitchen chairs and old sofas that have been stripped of their cushions. People waiting for the bus sit on an abandoned refrigerator that has been turned on its side. Herds of enormous water buffalo that produce milk for the area's famous mozzarella graze in the inland fields nearby. Random statues of the Virgin Mary dot the roadway. Some of the statues are adorned with flowers left to commemorate a road accident or a murder; one is overgrown with ditch weed, the virgin's head seeming to peek out from behind the tall grass.

On one wide corner that is especially popular for selling sex because it is an easy place for large trucks to stop, a Virgin Mary statue faces a burnt-out villa where three Nigerian women were burned to death, tied to their beds in the mid-2000s in what is believed to be a revenge killing by a madam when the women refused to sell sex. No one ever caught the perpetrators. It's unclear if anyone ever looked. Another statue a few miles down the road shows the Virgin Mary in prayer, her face towards the sky with her eyes closed.

As Sister Rita turns onto the Domitiana, flashes of the orange setting sun are visible through the ancient pines that separate the road from the seaside. A romantic would say the slivers of light look like a kaleidoscope; a realist knows the fiery sunset is more like the gates of hell. Down the road to the south, past Naples, is the Amalfi Coast with its popular tourist enclaves of Positano and Sorrento. To the north, Rome and its decadent grandeur are just over an hour away.

It is just before the hectic Holy Week leading up to Easter, and Sister Rita and her trusty assistant Sister Assunta are taking part in a springtime ritual of their own. For nearly twenty years, they and other nuns and volunteers have gone out to the Domitiana to offer what amounts to a chance for resurrection to the girls who are forced to stand on the streets day after day.

At any given time of the day or night, every single day of the year, no matter the weather, dozens of Nigerian women, some no older than high school age, line the road in various stages of undress. In the winter, they huddle over fires burning in oil barrels. In the summer, they try to stay cool under umbrellas. At night, the red brake lights of cars stopping makes the road look like a circus. Some men stop to pick them up; others just pull over to insult them.

The Domitiana has a troubled history. The ancient Roman road starts near Lake Avernus, a volcanic crater lake near a deep cave that ancient Romans believed was one of the entrances to

Hades' vast and sinister underworld. The road also winds past the Solfatara volcanic crater and its steaming white rocks at the center of the Phlegraean Fields, which is a super volcano that extends under the bay of Naples. In 2017, *Nature* warned that the "volcanic unrest" was reaching a "critical state."[21] The volcano could kill millions when it eventually does erupt, as it last did forty thousand years ago, which some scientists believe contributed to the extinction of the Neanderthals.[22] The super volcano is expected to blow anytime, which, considering the other more imminent threats, no one really seems to worry about.

By the late eighteenth century, the whole area around Castel Volturno had become a giant swampland. It was drained in the early 1940s under the order of Benito Mussolini as part of an experimental program to rid Italy of malaria. The experiment, during which the houses were sprayed in and out with DDT,[23] was conducted under the direction of the Rockefeller Foundation, which also ran a program to eradicate the disease from the island of Sardinia and across the southern Italian coast both before and after World War II.[24]

Twenty years later, in the 1960s, Vincenzo and Cristoforo Coppola, two enterprising brothers from Naples, bought a parcel of land along the seaside with the idea of building a utopian society designed to mimic Miami Beach.[25] Never mind that the area was a protected nature reserve, the flat beaches giving way to views of the sea were too good not to develop. The brothers' aim was to attract American military families who were stationed in Italy after the war. Their dream was to replace the sandy dunes and umbrella pine forests with a concrete city with its own ports, restaurants, church and school. In all, the Coppola brothers used more than thirty thousand square meters of concrete to realize their dream, which was an environmental nightmare, not to mention that it was illegally built with recycled Camorra crime money.

Nevertheless, the utopia was constructed with swanky restaurants, discotheques and a cinema to service the community who lived in dozens of large apartment blocks with views of Ischia from its crescent-shaped windows. The brothers built eight high-rise towers with scant windows facing the sea, which soon earned the nickname "eco monsters" by the locals. To keep the state off their backs for skirting building restrictions and destroying protected lands, they leased the towers for a token fee to NATO and the American military, which used them for office and housing facilities well into the late 1990s. When the brothers were accused of collusion with the Camorra, it became too hard to hide the fact that the Americans were essentially paying rent to a mafia organization.

Section by section, the compound was confiscated or condemned by the state with the intent of tearing down all the illegal structures and turning the village back into a nature reserve. Eventually, when the final lease with the Americans ran out in 2000, the state sequestered the entire beachfront property, vowing to level the eight tall towers, which hardly comprised the entire compound but which were the most symbolic to destroy. The Coppola brothers were fined for the illegal building and for destroying 150 species of fauna and flora native to the area. But in this part of Italy, few people go to jail, and the same Coppola brothers who built the settlement actually owned the company that won the contract to destroy the buildings, so their loss was also their gain.

The first of the towers was dramatically blown up with dynamite in 2001 in a move that was meant to show that organized crime was being defeated. People from all over the community came to watch and local anti-Mafia investigators cheered what was seen as a rare success. The remaining towers were razed two years later, but none of the other promises to revitalize the area have been kept yet, and instead the row of lower apartment blocks has become the perfect setting for the Camorra and Nigerian gangs to operate unchecked.

Because the Coppola buildings were stripped of all utilities when they were sequestered, those who refused to leave have had to improvise. The old black plumbing pipes are now used to drain sewage directly into the sea. Running water is stored in giant illegal holding tanks on some of the abandoned buildings, installed by Camorra companies that are well equipped to work around the system. Those who live in the condemned apartment blocks have also managed to string what look like spider webs of illegal electricity cables across the alleyways, tapped from the legitimate apartment blocks nearby.

A development called the Saraceno Park on the northern end of the village was also used as off-base housing for the American Navy until the mid-1990s. After the Americans left, it fell into disarray and is now so badly run down it has been condemned yet again by the state health officials because of rodents. Nigerians and homeless Italians now share the squalid space as squatters.

It is here, in front of these buildings that line the seafront promenade, that the nuns do battle for the souls of the girls. When the complex was built, the facades were terracotta orange to match the setting sun, but they are now pockmarked, the paint peeling in large chunks from years of neglect. Most of the half-moon windows have been stripped of glass, making them look like dark, half-open eyes squinting out at the polluted sea.

The area around Castel Volturno is easily the most lawless part of Italy. Those who live here say: "The only rule is that there are no rules."[26] Locals call it Beirut or the Bronx. Sergio Nazzaro, a local journalist who chronicles the insalubrious history of his city, refers to it as "Gotham City of the south, without Batman." Deals are made in blood, and murder rates are the highest in Italy, often topping a dozen a month. People disappear without a trace and no one ever looks for them. Nazzaro, who was born in Switzerland but grew up in Mondragone on the north end of the Domitiana, says criminality is such an integral part of the local society that people don't even realize what's legal and what is not. "Everyone is guilty," he tells me. But trying to stop the blatant criminality would open a Pandora's box and the local authorities don't want that. He says the area is also the Camorra's graveyard. "You can't imagine how many bodies are buried in fields and tied to rocks at the bottom of the river."

One of the reasons such degradation and lawlessness go unchecked is because of where it happens, in the heart of one of Italy's most corrupt regions. The Camorra run the crime syndicate in this area, and while Roberto Saviano's *Gomorrah* introduced some of the group's underworld activities to the world back in 2006, it offered very little in the way of new information for those who live around here. The whole area around Naples is known as *la terra dei fuochi* (Land of Fires), now too toxic to use for agriculture after years of rogue dumping of illegal waste at the hands of the Camorra. The Land of Fires is deadly in more ways than one. The region has the highest cancer rates in all of southern Europe, almost twelve percent above Italy's national average. Scores of people die every year from various tumors and lung diseases; eight children between the age of seven months and eleven years died of brain tumors over a twenty-day period in February 2017 alone. Stomach and liver cancer are also on the rise, no doubt from eating food still grown on the toxic land. A mobile chemotherapy unit patrols remote villages on a monthly basis to keep up with treatment for those who can't travel to Naples for care.

In 2014, Italy's agricultural ministry issued a report calling for a ban on the commercial sale of all products harvested from fields in a thirteen-square-mile area between Caserta, Castel Volturno and Naples.[27] It sent buffalo mozzarella lovers across the world into a tailspin, though the dioxin levels were found to be far less than in 2008, when the cheese was pulled from shelves worldwide following a similar ban. The result was that farm work became scarce, and

male migrant workers were quickly sucked into the underworld, either working for gangs from Nigeria and Ghana or
directly for the Camorra.

African migrants first started coming to the area in large
numbers in the 1980s to work in the tomato fields for cheap
wages. Italy was pouring money into the poor southern regions,
the Mezzogiorno, to try to boost the abandoned economy that
had been crippled by organized crime for as long as anyone
could remember. The end goal was to enable Italy to join the
European single currency market, which it could not do without investing in its poorest regions. This led many traditional
farm workers to move on to better paying factory jobs, which
opened up the migrant labor job market.

The Africans were not welcome to integrate with the Italians
and instead set up a peripheral society where they lived outside
the law, often squatting together in illegally built or unfinished
buildings. Italian authorities at the time did not pay much
attention to them, but they were not ignored by the Camorra
crime syndicate. Around this time, the Camorra was importing
its cocaine and heroin from South America, but as anti-narcotic
police in the Americas clamped down on transit routes, drugs
were increasingly routed through West Africa – and who better
to smuggle drugs from Africa than Africans, who soon brought
in their own criminal gangs to cash in.

Mostly men came at first, but by the 1990s, women started
arriving in greater numbers, too. They were rarely hired for farm
work, so many of the women felt they had no choice but to
prostitute themselves to survive. They were instantly popular,
attracting a flurry of Italian men looking for what was considered taboo sex with black women. Their sexual services were
also considerably cheaper than those offered by the Italian or
Eastern European prostitutes because Italian men didn't think
they had to pay black women the same as white women. They
were also in demand because many were young virgins who had
not been exposed to HIV/AIDS in Africa and they were thought

to be less risky than the European sex workers who were rumored to be carrying HIV. Many of those first prostitutes eventually became madams or pimps who were controlled by Nigerian gangs that needed to supplement their drug smuggling income to pay protection money to the Camorra to work on their territory.

As the demand for sex with black women grew, madams started trying to recruit more women from Nigeria to the area. When they wouldn't come willingly they soon started using traffickers to trick them into coming, eventually expanding the trade further north to Italy's larger cities and into Europe. The women were forced to dress in flashy costumes and parade up and down the streets, even though none of them wanted to sell sex. They were forced to get into cars and trucks with men and perform oral sex or hand jobs or have intercourse on the sides of the road. Eventually the madams used connection houses, but in the beginning most of the sex was outside and often included more than one man with one young woman.

Castel Volturno fast became a training ground where the girls were and still are being taught that if they resist, they will be gang raped or beaten. Soon many of the women brought over from Nigeria were sold to madams who had established territories further north in cities like Padova, Bologna and Turin. In Italy, Nigerian women are now forced to sell sex across the country, on busy boulevards and back roads in and around every major urban area, and many who were first forced into sex work in Italy now can be found as far away as the United Kingdom and Dubai, though most have a connection back to Castel Volturno.

It is a mistake to assume that all of these women have turned to selling their bodies because they couldn't find legitimate jobs or because they were desperate. Some surely have, but most are here because they were tricked. Other women in other places may choose sex work for a variety of reasons, but not the majority of Nigerian women on the Domitiana. They are not here by choice, they are trapped with nowhere to go unless someone saves them. And Sister Rita and her nuns cannot possibly save them all.

The key to the cycle that keeps the girls enslaved in plain view is the disturbing yet simple fact that the women and girls are told they owe exorbitant debts to their madams who helped get them to Italy. They pay it because they promised through the JuJu curse that they would do whatever their sponsor said they should or harm might come to them or their families, and they are told in convincing terms, mostly through threats of gang rape, that the only way they can pay off the sum is by selling their bodies.

Sister Rita knows many of the women who work on the Domitiana by name. She does not make them feel guilty for staying; she knows it's more than just a simple choice. So many of them are tied to the work due to the JuJu curse, and Sister Rita's bead of rosaries only goes so far in fighting that demon. Instead, she has to assure them that they will be safe if they leave, which is something she can only hope but not guarantee. Life in this part of Italy is extremely dangerous for the girls who live in the shadows and Sister Rita has seen too many tragedies to peddle false hope.

No one knows for sure how the stretch of road around Castel Volturno became ground zero for such blatant sex slavery. Some say it's proximity to Pompeii, where ancient lupanar rooms filled with erotic graffiti were thought to be brothels where slaves were forced to give their bodies to ancient Pompeian and Roman men in exchange for favors and food. Sex, it seems, has always been at a premium here.

The first time Sister Rita and her posse of nuns and volunteers came out to the Land of Fires was on International Women's Day on 8 March 1997, after the noticeable upswing in Nigerian sex workers started making local headlines. There had been a spate of car accidents along the Domitiana as men shopped for sex, and police were perplexed about what to do. Rather than clamp down on the trade, the local authorities constructed a series of roundabouts along the road to help manage the increased traffic.

The nuns were determined to get the women off the streets, no matter how dangerous it was for them. Sister Rita has no fear, often saying that the young girls out there in the dark waiting for perverted strange men are surely more terrified than she could ever be. The sisters had prepared little notes handwritten in English, Italian and French to give the girls, along with warm clothes and hot coffee. "Dear friend, with this gesture we want you to know that there is someone who thinks of you with love," the notes said, along with the address and phone number for Casa Ruth in Caserta. When they first started going out, the girls were shocked, remembers Sister Rita. "We were women meeting other women," Sister Rita said. "They were reduced to slavery. Slavery, which continues to compete with the drug and arms trade both for the turnover it produces and for the unscrupulousness of the methods and the organization that fuels it."

That first year, the nuns returned every two weeks to hand out the notes, coffee and even copies of the Qur'an. They did anything they could think of to convince the women and young girls to betray their madams and defy the ritual JuJu curse that keeps them in slavery thanks to the manipulative work of traffickers in Nigeria.

Things grew from there. After they had gone out to the street several times, the trafficked women started to trust them, and some even got into their car, emboldened by the sisters' promises of safety. Others came to the shelter in the middle of the night, walking miles to make their escape. The nuns started making inroads with the police, too, who started bringing the girls directly to the shelter when they went to the local station for help. Before that, women who asked for help were sent to jail, deported or ignored and sent back to the streets.

There is a tangible and constant underlying fear of death and bodily harm among the trafficked women, both on and off the streets. There is never a moment when they feel safe or relaxed. The anxiety eats away at many of them. Alcohol and drug dependency is a major problem among the African community in Castel Volturno, especially among the women who use these vices to cope. Sometimes when they are rescued from the streets, they require detox programs as well as psychological support. It is rarely a smooth transition from such dangerous work to safety.

Sister Rita is, in many ways, the quintessential nun, which is what makes her seem so out of place among the Nigerian women. Her flat grey hair is cut short and matches both her skin and the buttoned-up blouse she wears under her wool sweater, windbreaker, or puffy jacket, depending on the season. Her matching gabardine skirt falls below her knees, exposing tights that are so opaque they make her legs look like shiny cylinders that fit perfectly into her classic, thick-soled, black lace-up "nun shoes." In the summer, her legs are bare and she wears knock off Birkenstock-style sandals under her cotton skirt and short-sleeved blouse. She always wears a simple wooden cross around her neck. Sometimes she wears a nun's veil at mass. Sister Rita and the other nuns who work at Casa Ruth are one of the only rays of hope for getting the girls off the streets.

More than thirty thousand men and women from Nigeria and Ghana are thought to live in the town of Castel Volturno alone, according to the local city government, surpassing the size of the local population, which is estimated to hover around twenty-five thousand, according to the official census. That means undocumented migrants who don't pay taxes or utilize social services outnumber registered residents. Many have falsified documents that pass basic police checks and might get them medical care, although many more live like ghosts with no documentation at all.

It is well known that Nigerian sex slaves often disappear without a trace. No one knows if they've been sold to other madams or have been killed and disposed of. Sometimes their bodies are found in road ditches or ravines. Like the migrants at sea, they die nameless, buried without fanfare or often dumped in the local river. It is too dangerous for madams or even other women to report their deaths. Often, they are buried in the farmers' fields by friends who don't want to call attention to what happened. Some of the Nigerian women say that if a woman isn't bringing in enough money, her madam will kill her to teach a lesson to the others. The threat of death is omnipotent, but the threat of living the way many of these women have to live isn't necessarily a better option.

The feeling of impending danger is ever present in Castel Volturno. There is an uneasy silence that blankets what's left of the Coppola compound, broken only by an occasional distant cadence of popular American rap music streaming from open windows. It always feels as if someone is listening, watching. It's hard even to walk along the abandoned beach without the eerie feeling of being observed. The overpowering smell of dead fish, raw sewage that drains from the Coppola apartments, buffalo manure and rotting garbage adds to the overall uneasiness of the place. The fence that separates the sea from the squalor is piled high with garbage washed up by the waves on one side and littered by passersby on the other. Syringes and used condoms are tossed like candy wrappers on the broken sidewalks.

Children ride their bikes alongside rows of parked cars whose drivers are looking for illicit deals of one kind or another or just getting blow-jobs. The abandoned apartments are filled with Nigerians who run the sex, drugs and arms trade from the lower levels of the buildings. Most of the front entrances have been sealed by the police, but holes and openings in the fences make access easy enough. Some of the cordoned-off buildings even have Nigerian "doormen" to control who comes and goes. It is here in these buildings that the Camorra allows the Nigerian gangs to run one of the biggest cocaine trades in Europe, so long as they pay the syndicate a hefty monthly fee that is rumored to top sixty percent of their earnings.

Many of the villas that were built as single homes by the Coppola brothers are now used as "connection houses" by the Nigerian madams, who rent the rooms to the girls they own to bring their clients. Many of the trafficked women live and work in the same small rooms, often turning tricks twenty-four hours a day. The girls are everywhere – on every corner, standing behind trees on the side roads, waiting at bus stops.

Generally, Nigerian women are trafficked to Italy for sex in two ways – both of which are without consent and tragically similar to the old days of the slave trade. Either they are hand-picked, identified and "sold" directly from Nigeria through the use of recruiters and hidden Facebook pages with pictures to a madam who is already set up in Italy. In some cases, madams who are trying to establish their stable of women are known to travel across the sea with them to ensure they aren't "stolen" by other madams along the way. The second way they are trafficked is more general and entails traffickers selling the women directly to Nigerian gang members, who then sell them on to madams once they arrive in Italy.

Girls who are trafficked by men without a madam typically incur around €15,000 in travel expenses, including a cut to the recruiter or sponsor (like Joy's maman) in Nigeria and a cut to the smugglers for the price of the journey both across the desert and across the sea. Once they are sold to a madam in Italy, their costs go up to include the price the madam paid for them, usually around €5,000.

Girls who are trafficked directly to madams in Italy will owe far more, around €60,000. A cut goes to the recruiter in Nigeria, a cut to the traffickers and smugglers who expedited the women's journey and a large portion goes to the Nigerian gang members, who must pay the syndicates like the Camorra in whose territories the women will be forced to work. There are other incidentals along the way, including room, board, clothing and rent for the space on the sidewalk from which they will eventually solicit sex.

If we assume half of the girls who came to Italy in 2016 generated €60,000 each through debt bondage for the madams' gangs, the profits off those girls alone would top €300 million, even after their travel costs are deducted.

It can take up to five years or more of constant sexual slavery to pay off the massive debts. Then, women are free to go, but some end up becoming madams themselves, either brainwashed by what they perceive to be lucrative potential gains once their debts are paid or as an angry act of revenge: to bestow on others what they had to endure. This cycle has continued for more than a decade, but in 2016, the number of Nigerian women who arrived by smugglers' boats grew by sixty percent over the previous year.

Either way, all the women arrive with heavy debts before they even know they have been sold into sex slavery. Italy's anti-trafficking authorities estimate that there are as many as ten thousand Nigerian madams in operation in Italy, each with at least three women in their charge. Some of the madams also turn tricks to supplement their income, suggesting that they, too, are exploited.

Not everyone agrees on whether the women are aware of the fate that awaits them in Italy. I believe most don't, but some think all of them know exactly what to expect. I had a heated debate with journalist Nazzaro, who is convinced the women come from Nigeria by choice to work as prostitutes and that they aren't sex slaves at all. In his opinion, they see it as an enterprise and play the victim once they get caught. "They know exactly what they are doing," he says. Nazzaro is a parliamentary spokesman for the Five Star political movement, which shares staunch anti-immigration ideology with a lot of right-wing political parties in Europe, and doesn't buy the trafficking stories. "You can't tell me these women don't choose this. Look at how they dress and act," he says. "The only thing they don't know is how much money they have to give to their madams."

He believes that the stories of trafficking are grossly exaggerated by left-wing political parties who advocate open migration. "They don't owe you the truth, they will tell you whatever they think you want to hear," he tells me when I explain how many women I'd met who I was sure were true victims. "You can't know if they are lying. You don't speak their dialect, you can't take their word at face value."

When Sister Rita came to the Land of Fires, it was not like this. She and a group of nuns opened the Casa Ruth shelter in the city of Caserta, about an hour inland, in 1995 because it is the regional seat and one of the larger towns outside of Naples. Caserta has always had two faces. Tourists from all over the world come to Caserta to see its massive eighteenth-century Royal Palace, a UNESCO World Heritage Site that looms over a long ribbon of manicured gardens and artificial lakes. But the city is mostly known as a center for organized crime. So notorious is its reputation that *Sopranos* writers made it psychiatrist Jennifer Melfi's ancestral home.

Caserta is not as lawless as Castel Volturno, but it is hardly tranquil. Many tourist hotels in the area have armed guards and locked parking. The city just doesn't feel safe. There are always strange men lingering on the streets, always a sense that something bad is happening. It is too quiet. There is no sound of children laughing, no music coming from windows like in many other Italian towns of the same size.

Casa Ruth is on the Corso Trieste, one of the main avenues that cuts through the center of the town. At one end of the street is the monument to the fallen soldiers of World War I. At the other is the rear entrance of the Royal Palace. The sisters who run Casa Ruth belong to the order of Ursulines of the Sacred Heart of Mary, nuns that are well known for their charity to women and the poor. The first Roman Catholic nuns in the United States were Ursulines, having settled in New Orleans as part of a group of French immigrants from Normandy who came over on a five-month ocean voyage in 1727.

The shelter is named after the biblical figure Ruth, who was a convert to Judaism. Sister Rita says their community chose the name because it represents their aim at inclusiveness. She didn't want to open a "pre-packaged shelter for women." The situation in the Land of Fires was unique and needed a different kind of shelter.

Before coming down south to Caserta, Sister Rita lived in Vicenza, in the sophisticated, wealthy northern region of Italy, which is as far as one can get from the squalor of the Land of Fires. She arrived in Caserta with Sister Assunta and two other nuns in a green minibus on 2 October 1995. In her journal, she recalls a "magnificent sunset that stole our sights, alleviating the weight of the separation from home we carried in our hearts." Her journal was later published as the book *Slaves No More*, which continues to be sold to help raise funds for the shelter.

During their first years in Caserta, the Ursuline nuns quickly ran into difficulty carrying out their missionary work without a car. The city bus service was sporadic at best, not at all what they were used to in northern Italy, and walking proved impossible and dangerous. They soon acquired bicycles to get around, earning them a blip of relative fame that Sister Rita fondly remembers. The local newspaper ran a picture of her and another sister, describing them as "the bicycling nuns" who had arrived from the north. They cycled over the cobblestone streets, their habits flying in the wind, making their way around Caserta to visit women in prisons and hospitals. Eventually they bought a second-hand Fiat, which was stolen from them almost immediately, as were the next two Fiats with which they replaced it. They had a Rover that lasted for many years and now they drive a minivan with the Casa Ruth logo painted on the doors, which has, so far, detracted the thieves.

Casa Ruth's first live-in resident in 1997 was Atika, a woman born in Morocco who came to Italy with her husband on a rickety boat by way of Lampedusa. Atika's husband's illegal arms trade landed them both in jail, which is where she met Sister Rita, who back then combed the prisons in search of women who hadn't committed any crimes, of which there were many at the time, and who were imprisoned simply because authorities didn't know what else to do with them. Atika's husband was eventually deported back to Morocco, but Atika didn't want to join him and live under his oppressive rule after she tasted freedom while he was behind bars. Sister Rita helped Atika secure asylum and she stayed on and lived at Casa Ruth for a full year. Despite the fact that she was a practicing Muslim, Atika fit in well with the sisters, who used the experience to carve the path for what Casa Ruth would become, which is first and foremost a place where victimized women can learn self-respect. They realized through Atika's experience that women outside of Europe are often brainwashed and more inclined to defer to men as their protectors. Many truly believe women are not free to make their own choices.

"She helped us build a connection," recalls Sister Rita. "A Muslim woman among the nuns – we were united like true sisters."

The shelter has taken many forms over the years, sometimes occupying space in the back rooms of the rectory, other times in borrowed apartments. Now they are finally in a permanent space owned by the local diocese. The shelter comprises three first-floor apartments, the walls between them knocked down. The space feels informal and haphazard, not at all institutional. It is somewhat fitting for the chaos of these women's lives, and they seem to feel at ease there. You reach the entrance through a private access from the courtyard, so no one has to meet anyone in the building's hallways. It is discreet, private and perfect in many ways.

A covered terrace offers some respite from the humid summers, but there is little natural light inside the building except from the windows in Sister Rita's study and the chapel. The apartment complex houses mostly elderly people who weren't so keen to have a shelter for rescued sex slaves as a neighbor, at least at first – Sister Rita has since won them over, even successfully recruiting some as volunteers.

Most of the rooms are set up with single beds and baby cribs dressed with bright, colorful linens. Others feature bunk beds and African art.

A massive wooden crucifix draped with a rosary hangs on the main wall in front of a small wooden altar in the airy chapel, which is in the living room of one of the former apartments. African paintings and colorful posters with prayers decorate the sidewalls. A sheer, white curtain hangs over the window, casting a pearly light on the white tile floor.

Prayer rugs are rolled up in the corner for the many Muslim women who find themselves here. Several copies of the Qur'an line a small shelf by the door. It is no coincidence that the crucifix hangs on the wall facing Mecca. When the babies who live in the shelter take their afternoon naps, the nuns roll their buggies up next to the altar.

"It is easily the quietest and most peaceful room in the entire shelter, and the babies sleep peacefully in here," Sister Assunta explains.

Sister Assunta is an older, softer version of Sister Rita, with a rounder face and smoother skin. She has a wonderful sense of humor and a contagious smile, and she defers to Sister Rita for all matters, though she is not without strong opinions of her own. Her biggest nemeses are the male clients, whom she says are the real problem. She hates the men who pay for sex, and she is quick to criticize anyone who dismisses their role in this racket, often saying that without them there would be no need for what she and Sister Rita do.

The youngest woman I ever met at Casa Ruth was a teenager called Betsy, whose vacant eyes still haunt me. She didn't look like the other Nigerian girls, and Sister Rita suspected that she might have been from Somalia, though she didn't talk enough for us to get much of a family history. Her double-take looks made her especially vulnerable on the Domitiana, where men tend to seek out women they could never have sex with through normal channels. But she was young and she didn't know to insist that her clients wear condoms, and she soon ended up pregnant.

Her baby was just two months old when I first met Betsy, when I was visiting Casa Ruth for lunch one day. She was sleeping quietly in a baby stroller at the end of the table, seemingly oblivious to the laughter of the other children playing on the floor nearby. When the baby, whom the sisters called Faith because Betsy didn't want to name her, did finally cry, Sister Rita hopped up to comfort and rock her so Betsy could eat. Betsy was extremely thin despite having just given birth. She seemed in a state of shock, often drifting off into a trance-like state or just staring straight ahead.

Betsy barely spoke Italian, though Sister Rita tried desperately to teach her, hoping she could reach her somehow. Every time Sister Rita tried to touch her arm to comfort her, Betsy flinched and pulled it away. Later, I learned that she was systematically beaten and raped by her madam's henchmen when she refused to come on to men on the Domitiana. Eventually, she stopped eating and passed out on the street. The police picked her up and brought her straight to Casa Ruth. It was only there that she discovered she was nearly six months pregnant. Sister Rita was worried she might be suicidal, but the birth of Faith seemed to have brought her around, ever so slightly.

After she had finished picking at her food, Betsy plucked Faith from Sister Rita's arms and swaddled her in a long African print scarf which she tied onto her back. She then walked up and down the halls of the shelter, humming an African lullaby.

The women at Casa Ruth speak Nigerian Pidgin, which is a conglomeration of various African dialects and the English language. It is a language Sister Rita does not speak, though at times it seems quite clear that she understands it. She tries to teach them Italian instead. Usually, when women first come to the shelter, the only words they know in Italian are terms for blow-jobs and sexual positions, which makes for unusual conversation between the nuns and the women. But Sister Rita cannot be shocked – she has heard and seen it all. They initially communicate using universal hand signs for sleepy, thirsty, hungry and other basic needs. Then one of the other women who speaks Italian translates each newcomer's story so the nuns can try to determine what personal boundaries or special needs the women have. Some women need to share their horrible journeys; others suppress them.

One of the things they do best at the shelter is making sure every woman living there feels empowered enough to be part of the team to save those who have just arrived. When they know new women are coming, they meet to pray and discuss a strategy to welcome them, complete with contingency plans, including what to do if they have been severely abused or if they are thought to have an STD or are pregnant. When women just show up on their doorstep, everyone improvises.

Since communication is vital, Sister Rita has taped small white labels to all the furniture in the shelter, each of which has an Italian description written on it in black marker. They are meant to help teach the residents basic Italian words, like *culla* (baby crib) and *armadio* (closet). It is reminiscent of a kindergarten classroom.

There is a main kitchen for the shelter and a side kitchen where the girls can make tea or warm up baby bottles. Depending on the makeup of the group at any given time, sometimes all the girls each cook their own meals and eat when they want to as a way to avoid fights and arguments. Other times, or when there are visitors, they eat together like a big family of women and babies. Some people stay for many months; others just a few days.

Perhaps no two groups of women could seem more opposite than elderly white Italian virgin nuns and young Nigerian black women who have been forced to sell their bodies to anonymous men for lurid sex acts. They have a strange kind of mismatched kindred spirit, and their bonds defy all logic, at least at first. But it was the English cardinal Vincent Nichols, the man Pope Francis appointed to lead an anti-trafficking initiative called the Santa Marta Group, who explained perfectly how the nuns gain the trust of the Nigerian women and vice versa.

Sitting on an ornate red tapestried settee in the English College on the Via Giulia in Rome, a far cry from the streets of the Domitiana, he explained that the reason the two groups of women bond so easily is because, contrary to what we might think, they harbor no preconceived notions about each other. "The nun cannot envision the prostitute's journey any more than the prostitute can envision the nun's," he said. "That's why they find their common ground as women. Their trust in each other is pure because they have no reason not to trust each other."

There is no sense of judgment whatsoever by the nuns towards the girls. Even when they first come into the shelter, even when they are treated for STDs or when they can't possibly pinpoint who the fathers of their babies are. Nor do they ask too many questions when the women have extra pocket money or when they suddenly disappear when they aren't scheduled to be gone. There is no place for suspicion in the business of saving souls. The nuns are on the front line of a dangerous battle with very few allies and they can't afford to doubt anyone's sincerity.

They know the women are afraid. They know they are embarrassed and humiliated by what they've been through. The nuns work to give them back a sense of dignity that the madams took from them.

"You can't imagine what they have to do," Sister Rita once told me. "They are forced, out of fear they will be killed or beaten, to show affection towards these men. They have to satisfy them. They have to pretend they enjoy it or the client might not pay. It's the lowest form of humiliation."

Sister Rita tries to counsel the women to love themselves. Those who are pregnant are sometimes easier to work with because the baby becomes a distraction. They can be encouraged to be kind to themselves "for the baby" and are told not to be depressed or it might hurt the pregnancy. Sister Rita believes that all women have an innate maternal instinct and that even under these horrific circumstances of conception a woman can love a baby she is carrying. And, perhaps more importantly, that the baby will love them back, unconditionally. "Many of these girls don't know what to expect when they give birth, but when their baby needs them, they sometimes feel loved for the first time in their lives," she says. "And they can't help but love those babies back. That love saves them."

It's much harder for the victims of sexual exploitation to forgive themselves. Many women who are forced into prostitution develop serious body image issues. Some become anorexic. Some self-mutilate. They see themselves as unattractive or even disfigured. Sister Rita does not have mirrors in any of the sleeping rooms at Casa Ruth. Sometimes it takes a long time before they are ready to look at themselves. Sometimes the ability never comes.

There are many misconceptions when it comes to the worldliness of the nuns and what they understand. When I first started working on this project, I assumed that the celibate nuns would have no way to relate to what the Nigerian women had gone through because they weren't sexually active themselves.

But as I got to know more victims, I realized that no woman can relate to sexual slavery unless she has lived it because the choices these women must make and the acts that those who are victims are forced to perform cannot be equated to any aspect of sex as most women know it.

In the case of the sex trafficked women, especially the young ones, the act of sex is rape. They dread it, hate it, and loathe the men who pay for it and despise their madams who force them to do it. In that sense, there is no difference between a virginal nun and a married mother of two when it comes to relating to what these women have gone through. We simply can't.

There are degrees of empathy, sympathy and skepticism that go with the study of this sort of tragedy. Many times when I met women who had been rescued or who had escaped their madams and yet chose to dress in sexy or tight clothing, I found myself second-guessing them. It took a long time to realize that recovery for many women includes the right to feel sexy without fear of exploitation, to feel pretty without being judged and to feel happiness without any guilt. The problems of perception almost always start with those of us on the periphery, not those at the epicenter.

While they might not comprehend the full horror that the women have been through, the nuns truly feel that they are conduits to God for those they are helping. In their eyes, only God can help them defy the JuJu curse and forgive themselves. In a perfect world, the women would get psychiatric counseling to help deal with the trauma they've been through, but those sorts of services are not available in the Land of Fires, so the nuns have to fulfil multiple roles. There is simply no one else even trying to help.

It is impossible to appreciate truly just what nuns on the front line of a crisis like this are faced with. They do daily battle with few rewards, risking their lives at the hands of one of the deadliest organized crime syndicates in the world. At Casa Ruth, the happiest days are those when babies are born or brought home from the hospital, but even those days must surely be clouded by the circumstances. There are moments of laughter and celebration, but it would be a stretch to describe a single day at Casa Ruth as one filled with a natural joy. Every day is just a different degree of tragic.

The nuns have an easier time trusting the girls they save than the other way around. Because so many of the women forced into sexual slavery were duped by what they thought were religious women back home, the nuns at Casa Ruth have more to prove. It is unbelievably common to hear that the first point of contact for the women who end up being trafficked to Italy was at a local mosque or church in Nigeria, when a religious-seeming woman asked them about their life. Those first conversations, all so similar no matter where the girls were from, serve as a sort of screening for the recruiters. Eventually, the faux-religious women gain their trust under the auspices of shared worship or through a common perceived desire to find a better life. Soon, the religious woman in Nigeria has an idea, a cousin or brother in Europe who needs a babysitter, a friend with a beauty salon who needs a braider. The story is almost always the same, so when the nuns first approach the women, it is understandable that the girls are skeptical.

Sister Rita knows that obstacle all too well. "We have to give them time to see we are here to help," she says. "They see that we are dressed as nuns, we act like nuns, and I think that helps. We also have a reputation among the women on the Domitiana. We are known as a place to help, if only they can get to us."

The sisters run the shelter on a tight schedule, even though they are often disrupted by new arrivals and basic problems inherent in southern Italy. Mornings are spent shuttling the women and girls to activities. Some of the women work as cleaners in nearby office buildings or private houses, some are studying for their high school exams in Italian. Someone almost inevitably has a doctor's appointment for an STD that just won't go away or a prenatal or postnatal check-up.

Sister Rita drives the girls to their appointments and even holds their hands as the doctors examine them. That way, she says, she can ensure the girls will be treated with the respect that is often spared on migrants, especially Africans.

"They don't like to be touched," Sister Rita told me once after taking a young woman to a doctor visit. "Some of them have serious post-traumatic stress disorder from all the rapes and beatings and sex."

The babies at Casa Ruth are the saviors and the elderly sisters are natural grandmothers to them. Before the era of Pope Francis, children born out of wedlock were never actually denied the rite of baptism, but it was done discreetly. The Church didn't want to punish the child, but it also did not want to be seen to approve of the way it was conceived. Now, under Pope Francis, babies are more likely to be baptized in celebration, whether they are born of prostitutes, same-sex couples or the traditionally married whom the Church prefers. Sister Rita had been celebrating baptisms in the local church long before Francis normalized them. By recognizing the babies like that, she hopes that the young mothers will accept them, too.

"It's not their fault," she says. "These babies need all the support they can get. There are few babies in the world born of such unloving circumstances."

Once, when I was at Casa Ruth for lunch, Sister Rita and I waited in the dining room with a few of the children whose mothers were not yet back from their morning activities. While we waited, she picked up eleven-month-old Emanuele, whose mother was at an Italian lesson. She figures he is the sixtieth baby that has come through the shelter in the last few years, though it is hardly cause for commemoration.

Emanuele's skin is much lighter than his mother's and Sister Rita explains that the fathers of these babies are surely Italian because they are the only clients who pay double not to have to use a condom. But that's as much as anyone will ever know about Emanuele's father, or the rest of the babies she has helped bring into the world.

Emanuele squeals with laughter and starts pounding on Sister Rita's chest, wrapping his tiny fingers around the wooden cross that hangs around her neck. Soon Emanuele jumps down and scampers across the floor – he has been walking since he was just nine months old, she tells me proudly. Sister Rita then shows me the walls of the dining room, which are plastered with snapshots of all the babies she and the sisters have saved. Each photo has been lovingly cut into hearts and diamonds and glued onto colored paper.

There are scant photos of their mothers, who find it hard to smile, she says. When I ask her more about what will happen to the babies, she tells me that they are the most unwanted children she has ever known. They are the product of sex trafficking, or rape, and though not begotten of love, she reminds me, her thin finger in the air, they deserve to be treated as if they were.

Emanuele's mother Beauty soon returns from her Italian lesson and takes Emanuele to change his diaper. She was forced into sex slavery through the all-too-common initiation rite of a violent gang rape more than three years before her son was born. Her thick hair has been braided into dozens, maybe even hundreds, of narrow cornrows, clearly done by one of the other women in the house who likely thought that she was coming to Italy to work as a braider in a salon. Some of the braids are laced with orange ribbons; others are attached to lighter colored extensions. The perfect braids are tied into a ponytail that is perched high on the left side of Beauty's head, giving her a touch of innocence and whimsy. She is quick to smile, one of the few women who actually looks happy. In fact, she looks like any college-aged student you might see almost anywhere else in the world.

Later on, the women and babies and nuns gather in the dining room. A large steaming dish of African rice and spicy tomato sauce has been prepared by one of the women who left the shelter several years ago, but who now works for the nuns as their cook and cleaner.

"This is Honey. She is a real success story," Sister Rita tells me as she cups the young woman's face in her hands. "She is married now and has four beautiful children."

Honey looks at Sister Rita and smiles warmly.

"Mamma saved me," she tells me. All the women and girls at Casa Ruth call Sister Rita "mamma," which is a term of respect Nigerians often use for women who are older them.

We all stand as Sister Rita begins the lunchtime prayer of thanks, followed by a quick sign of the cross and then the scraping of the wooden chairs across the tile floors as everyone tucks into the meal. The sisters pour themselves small glasses of tart red wine from a dark bottle emblazoned with the Ursuline crest.

None of the young women drink. Emanuel eats a few bites of rice as he sits on his mother's lap and then makes his way around the table while she eats. He is a happy child, so blissfully unaware of the misery that brought him into being.

Later, I ask Sister Rita if the children will ever know about their mothers' lives. "That's up to them," she tells me. "Hopefully not. You know, a little white lie never hurts."

Then she smiles in a way that makes you wonder whether she is serious or not, a trait as endearing as it is unnerving. Her keen wit, both ironic and astute, must be how Sister Rita squares all she has to do to save these women and still keep her faith.

She describes one of the first women she helped off the street, whose daughter later found out she was forced into sex work. "This woman's daughter went to her one day and asked why she had stayed at Casa Ruth, because that's a place for whores," Sister Rita says, shaking her head in sadness. The woman's daughter never accepted it, and the two became estranged. "These women pay for the crimes of others their whole life."

And not everyone fits in. In 2016, they opened their doors to a Ukrainian woman who was part of a growing network of non-Nigerian women who are trying to cash in on the local Domitiana sex market. At first, Sister Rita thought she was "pure of heart," which is generally all it takes to qualify to stay. But soon the nuns realized the woman had fallen in love with one of her clients and was hoping to break up his marriage. Apparently, she would meet him at a hotel nearby. Casa Ruth provided the perfect cover for their illicit relationship and paid the woman's expenses so she wouldn't have to prostitute herself to other men. Eventually the sisters kicked her out. "She didn't want to follow our path to serenity," Sister Assunta explained. "We have no place for those who won't walk with us here."

At the end of each day, the women who live at Casa Ruth put their babies to bed and Sister Rita makes a final walk around the shelter, picking up stray toys and straightening the pictures on the walls. Sometimes she sits in the dark kitchen wondering and worrying about what is going to happen when she and the other sisters are too old to do this work. She feels twenty years younger than she is, she says, but there may be a time when the babies and tragedy become too much for her.

"I hope a younger sister will come join us to learn about what we do," she tells me before she heads off to bed. "I worry that the shelter won't continue if we leave."

Nights are short at Casa Ruth, filled with noise. Babies cry, and sometimes so do the women. Whispers turn to giggles or arguments. Other times someone sings or hums African lullabies as they walk their babies up and down the hallways. In the morning, Sister Rita is the first to rise and the smell of the first drops of espresso coffee from the worn-out Moka pot is like an olfactory alarm clock. The shelter slowly wakes up to face another day that will have laughter and tears. It is most terrifying to think about what would happen if it weren't here.

A man with a live chicken, used in black magic rituals, cycles along the Domitiana on his way to a witch doctor who will place a JuJu curse on a trafficked woman to tie her to her madam.

3

MADAMS AND THE BLACK MAGIC JUJU CURSE

"The curse cannot be broken. Not even prayer can get rid of the JuJu." – Rose, sex trafficking victim

NAPLES – The first time I met Rose was in the dining room at Casa Ruth. She is a petite woman who wears her hair in an intricately styled Afro that she constantly adjusts and pushes into place as she speaks. She has a thick raised scar that cuts a white diagonal line across her dark forehead down through her left eyebrow. It is from a bottle that her madam broke over her head at a connection house in Castel Volturno.

Rose took part in a black magic JuJu ritual before she left Benin City, but she doesn't like to talk about it in detail because she still believes it could bring her harm. She is visibly nervous at the very mention of it. She says that she had too many bad experiences not to believe in the curse. She says the JuJu is still inside her. "The curse cannot be broken," she whispers. "Not even prayer can get rid of the JuJu."

She doesn't like Sister Rita hearing her talk about the fear she still has, and she will not share a single detail of her particular ritual or the witch doctor who performed it. "I can't. Talking about it will wake the JuJu, so don't ask me any more," she pleads. Rose likes to hold the hands of people she is talking to and her hands are always ice cold and clammy, which she says is because of the curse and how the spirit has deadened some of her soul.

Fear of and belief in the curse is a secret that all the women keep from the sisters at Casa Ruth. It's better if the nuns believe they've left the black magic behind. The girls won't even discuss it inside the shelter. Rose says they are afraid it will capture the nun's good heart if they even bring it up. "Sister Rita is such a good woman," Rose says. "She has God in her and the JuJu feels it when she is near, but no one is completely safe."

Rose did know that she might end up in sex work when she came to Italy back in 2011. She had heard rumors of the sort in Nigeria, but had hoped it wouldn't happen to her. In any case, she didn't think she was attractive enough with her short, robust stature. Instead, she thought that she was coming to Italy to continue her work as a hairdresser and braider, which was her profession in Benin City. The JuJu ritual, she thought, was just a promise to pay back those who helped arrange her journey once she started earning money. Her parents even cobbled together what money they had to send with her. They viewed it as an investment so that she could soon start sending money home to help them.

In a village in Nigeria's poor Edo State, a family can live comfortably for €200 a month, and Rose thought she would surely be making at least that every week in Italy. Like so many of the other victims, she also met a woman who told her she could help her get to Europe through her church group. This woman is the one who arranged the JuJu curse, which was performed as soon as Rose was told that there was work for her in Italy.

Rose came to Italy when Gaddafi still held power in Libya, before sex trafficking was the lucrative business it is today. She was among a growing number of Nigerian women coming into the country under a system that was different from what it is now. She had to pay smugglers for her own transportation costs, which were mild by comparison to what they are today. She was able to move quickly across the Sahara Desert and didn't run into any trouble to speak of in Libya beyond the regular inconveniences that go with such an underworld journey.

When Gaddafi was still in charge, the rampant kidnappings and brutal detentions weren't part of the migrant trail like they are now. People didn't die waiting to cross, but they did perish at sea in far greater numbers than they do today. Libya was a police state where many things happened outside of the norms of international law, but it wasn't lawless.

In Libya, Rose paid all the money her family saved for her to a smuggler for the sea voyage to Lampedusa on a rickety boat. She estimates that it was around $1,000 (approx. €900), although she can't be sure because at the time she didn't know simple math or the value of money. Now the voyage can cost €7,000 or more per person. Because Rose came to Italy long before Mare Nostrum and the charity boats started carrying out active rescues, she came on an old fishing boat that had to make it all the way to the island, which these boats generally did by crashing straight into the rocks. The ship she was on was at sea for more than a week before they finally wrecked on the shore. Like Joy who traveled across the desert, they had no food or water and they had to drink their own urine to survive.

The Italian Coast Guard knew in advance when boats were on the way to Lampedusa, but back then nobody thought to rescue them. The 2011 film *Terraferma* depicts the way it used to be, when fishing vessels couldn't even help those on sinking migrant boats they came upon out of fear their boats would be sequestered and their crew charged with abetting illegal immigration.

People died so frequently that bodies often washed up on the Italian shores, and fishermen caught skulls and bones in their nets so often that they just threw them back into the sea rather than spending the time it would take to report the discovery of a body part. It wouldn't have been of much use even if they had, anyway, since smuggler ships don't have passenger lists and the dead are rarely identified.

I showed Rose some old pictures that I had kept on my phone of the smuggler-ship graveyard on Lampedusa, which is stacked high with the carcasses of hundreds of old smugglers' boats that were hauled off the shoreline. She swiped through them with the nostalgia one might have when looking through vacation pictures. "Is it this one?" she said, enlarging the picture to get a good look at the wreck. "No, maybe it's the one behind it."

Within a month of arriving in Italy, Rose was in Castel Volturno working two different patches of sidewalk, one in the morning and the other in the afternoon. She stayed on the streets for three long years. Men often refused to pay her, telling her that she wasn't attractive enough to get paid for sex. She was frequently beaten by her madam when she worked all day and didn't bring in enough money. Her eyes swell with tears when she recounts how the clients often forced her to do degrading acts, beating her when she refused.

The sex acts forced upon Nigerian women are made all the more degrading because they often involve men who do not wash before picking up the girls. I have been told by many women that they carry around wet wipes and ask the men to clean themselves before they will perform oral sex, but many refuse because there is a sick pleasure in forcing a woman to put her mouth on an unclean penis. Hand jobs are also common, with women being forced to let the men ejaculate in their mouths. Full intercourse is less common, in part because it is more expensive and entails going to a connection house or finding an area outside. Men who pay for sex often do not wish to have sex in their cars out of fear they will make a mess that their wives or girlfriends might find. Women told me stories of intercourse turning into anal rape, or how men insert objects like tree branches or metal pipes into their anuses or vaginas.

Many of the clients who pay for intercourse do ask for anal sex, which is something not all girls concede to, and certainly something they charge more for if they do. Some of the sex slaves who are forced to turn up to twenty tricks or more a day admit to applying a deadening cream to their vagina or anus so they don't feel anything at all. More than one woman has mentioned an injection like Botox that can be self-administered, essentially to make repetitive sex less painful.

Dolly, the window girl in Amsterdam whom I met in Lampedusa in 2011, said she eventually got off the streets in Italy because so many of the men in northern Italy wanted threesomes or were sadomasochistic and used bondage or filmed the acts and then posted the encounters on social media porn sites. "I didn't want a film out there," she said. "What if I have children some day and they find it?"

The scars on Rose's body are like a roadmap of the hell she has endured. Cigarette burns from one client, a bent and broken pinkie finger from another. Rose's story seemed especially brutal. But when I asked Sister Rita why Rose was so unlucky and why she had so many more scars from her ordeal than the other women, she corrected me. The only difference between Rose and the others was that the other women don't talk about or show their scars.

Rose lived in a rundown connection house off the Via Domitiana, where she would bring men from the street. The house was in the complex of single-story villas built for the Coppola Village estate, but no one had ever lived there, so there were no appliances and the plumbing was very basic, with a toilet that had no seat on it and just one sink that they used for cooking and bathing. A thin tube was attached to the sink since there was no shower stall or bathtub. The villa had no heating and in the winter months they had to use a propane heater that sometimes sparked and caught the curtains on fire.

The kitchen was set up as a sort of bar with cocktails and some snacks locked up in cabinets. Her madam sometimes had parties in the connection house, inviting Nigerian men who would come for shots of whiskey or vodka or other liquor and then pay extra to take girls to the back bedrooms. The charge for Nigerian clients was far less than what they could charge white men, so the drinks were a way many of the madams made up for the low prices. It was not uncommon for a few madams to throw these parties together, bringing other women to the house, which meant many of them used the beds for sex and then slept in the same beds on the party nights, even though they only had one set of sheets that had to be washed by hand and left to dry in the wind.

She said sometimes she worked twenty-four hours a day, often turning a dozen or more tricks without sleeping. Her goal was to pay off her madam, but she somehow never got ahead.

Rose wasn't formally educated in Nigeria and although she could recognize letters and read some simple words, she was not skilled at all in math. As a result, she had no accurate means to keep track of the money she paid to her madam. She had no choice but to trust that her madam was correctly deducting her earnings from her debt, which should have been less than the usual €60,000 since she paid her own transportation. But whenever she asked, it seemed she had been charged for more clothes or rent or food and she never caught up. She had no basis from which to argue, however, because she didn't really understand the numbers. Many of the women keep their own tallies of their debts, but Rose could not.

Eventually, she fell in love with a young Nigerian man whom she met at an underground party in Castel Volturno Destra, the part of town where most Africans live, held at a former pizzeria where Africans would gather to share traditional music and food. These parties are different to the parties at the connection houses. No money is exchanged and no one has sex unless they want to.

Rose's boyfriend knew what she did for a living, and while he didn't judge her for it, they had understandable issues with intimacy at the beginning of their relationship. Yet, she was able to develop a deep emotional connection to him over time, which allowed her to trust a man in a way few women in her position ever do.

Rose's boyfriend was also bound by the JuJu curse. The ritual used on men is slightly different from the one women take part in and often includes flagellation and other forms of self-torture. He was recruited as a drug mule for the Nigerian gangs after his asylum was denied while he was staying at CARA Mineo. He was from Borno State in the north of Nigeria and had left to avoid being recruited by Boko Haram militants who had convinced many of his friends to join their cause in its infancy, long before they gained notoriety by abducting the Chibok girls in 2014. He was denied asylum in 2012 and given ten days to leave Italy, but the authorities didn't give him any financial support or a plane ticket to do so.

As he was plotting how to get back to Nigeria, he met a man who told him that he knew about a job in Castel Volturno where he could eventually get legal documents to stay in Europe. The man gave him a phone number and told him to go to the city of Catania where a friend would help him get hold of a job. In Catania, he met many other Nigerian men as well as many men from Ghana who were also denied asylum and trying hard to make a plan to stay in Europe.

Many of them wanted to try to get to France where there are far more African communities to disappear into than exist in Italy. Some of the men ended up taking the train to Ventimiglia on the border between Italy and France near the French and Italian Riviera, close to Nice. From there they were told they could hire men who would take them across the border through the mountains if they couldn't cross by train. Rose's boyfriend didn't want to go to France, so he waited around until a man came to take them to Castel Volturno. Once there, he was given a job running drugs from one crack house to another on an old bicycle. At first, he had to wrap the drugs in packets around his legs until he understood how to recognize cops and other threats, including rival gang members who might steal his precious cargo. Eventually, he carried the drugs in a backpack.

Rose and her boyfriend left the Via Domitiana together after she became pregnant with their daughter. But not before Rose was beaten senseless by her madam, who was angry with her for not being more careful. Rose forced her clients to use condoms by lying about being HIV positive. In order to separate the act of paid sex from the intimacy she shared with the man she loved, she didn't use a condom with her boyfriend, she says, even though she knew the risk of pregnancy was high. Her madam told her to keep working during the pregnancy, saying she could take some time off after the delivery. She would arrange for a babysitter, but, of course, Rose would have to pay extra for that.

The thought of raising a baby in a connection house where she was forced to have sex with strangers in the next room was unacceptable to her, so she made a plan with her boyfriend to run away.

Once Rose and her boyfriend escaped the Domitiana, however, her battle was far from over. Her boyfriend took a job as a bricklayer at a construction company run by the Camorra near Caserta and Rose stayed at Casa Ruth until their baby, Faith (a common name for babies born under Sister Rita's watch), was born, in part to try to improve her reading and learn simple math. Eventually, Rose found a job with a company that provided cleaning services for an American military base near Caserta. The nuns and other women took care of Faith at Casa Ruth while she worked.

But the people running the company that cleaned for the Americans were corrupt – and mean. Rose was beaten, verbally abused and paid slave wages for excruciating work under often-dangerous, toxic conditions. She finally left the cleaning company, but not before her manager threatened to kill her and her baby. Rose left anyway. As she tells it, this is the work of the JuJu inside her soul for betraying her madam.

Shortly after leaving the cleaning company, Sister Rita convinced Rose to start working at the New Hope Cooperative, which is a sewing shop run by Casa Ruth to help sustain the women rescued from the streets. She and her boyfriend eventually moved into a small one-room apartment in the center of Caserta and they plan to get married one day. Sister Rita has pushed Rose to challenge herself, telling her that she will only succeed if she takes safe risks. To do that, Sister Rita is training her to run the till at the boutique. Several months after I first met Rose, I returned to New Hope and bought a hand-sewn notebook cover made from dark-green fabric that came with a green pen with the New Hope logo. Rose counted my money and gave me the change and carefully wrote out a receipt as Sister Rita looked on with the pride of a mother whose child had just graduated from Harvard.

Still, Rose worries about the JuJu curse. She has become a devout Christian and she has tried to replace the fear of the spirits she believes still possess her with faith. But even that is difficult. Her eyes well with tears again as she explains that she hopes all the gods will forgive her for what she has done – the JuJu "god" for breaking the curse, and her Christian god for what she says are her sins of selling her body on the street.

But the worst part of Rose's story is that she still plans to pay her madam back one day, even though she is free from the slavery that kept her on the street. It is common for women who escape the streets to continue to feel the weight of the financial burden, often convinced they still owe the hefty debts or something terrible will happen to them because of the JuJu. "That's the only way to really break the curse," Rose says. "How can I not pay the debt?"

Using the curse to exploit vulnerable women is a genius scheme that works thanks to the Nigerian madams, who are skilled at manipulation, because they, too, were almost always victims themselves. They know what works best.

In any other circumstance, it would seem absurd if someone produced a bill for €60,000 that could only be paid back in €10 hand jobs, €15 blowjobs and €25 intercourse. But somehow the victims truly believe that they owe that much, and not even for the privilege to live freely; they pay that much to live like prisoners and slaves. Part of the misconception is that they see Europe, even their prison-like conditions in the dirt-poor city of Castel Volturno, as advanced. There are basic amenities like running water and electricity that many didn't have back home. This seems to skew their perception of what being here is worth.

The madams, too, convince the women that heat and electricity and running water are outrageously expensive. It is impossible for the victims of trafficking to understand just how inflated the cost of living they are charged for really is. But what is most heartbreaking is how many women simply accept what they are told. It underscores their vulnerability and the damage poverty and manipulation have done to their resolve as human beings. They lose confidence and, with it, often their perspective about what anything is worth, including themselves. They are tied to both the curse and the lies that accompany it.

The JuJu ritual varies depending on the black magic doctor performing it, but invariably includes some form of animal sacrifice, a promise of obedience, threats against the womb and the swearing of one's soul as collateral for eventual debt.

Some women are forced to eat still-beating chicken hearts cut and torn from the live fowl in front of them. Others witness or even take part in the bloodletting of goats and are then either coerced to drink the blood or directed to prance around smoldering rocks with the dead animals on their back, the warm blood running down their spine. Some witchdoctors use sharp razors to remove parts of the women's nipples or tufts of their pubic hair to leave in Nigeria. The scars left by the cuts are filled with dirt to bind them to their homeland. Most women are forced to leave a package of their body bits in Nigeria, which they are convinced can be used to control them from afar.

Many women are shaved from head to toe. Others have to ingest a mixture of their own toenails, hair or menstrual blood. The curse ties them to the priest who performs it, who then transfers that power over them to the mamans in Nigeria who recruit them for the sex trade, and then those mamans give the power to the madams in Italy who will eventually pimp them.

JuJu is often incorrectly considered the same as voodoo, which is a form of "white magic" in many African cultures. Despite its sinister connotations in popular culture, voodoo is generally thought to be used to help people. JuJu, on the other hand, is strictly sinister and meant only to harm. Both practices play on superstitions and fear, which makes them harder to break since those under the spell tend to associate anything untoward that happens to them with the JuJu itself. When women on the street in Castel Volturno have any sort of psychological problem, the other women assume it is the JuJu curse at work.

The curse is usually administered in Nigeria before the women depart, but there are at least two witch doctors that perform the curse in Castel Volturno. One makes house calls to the connection houses where new arrivals and non-compliant women live. The other works out of the ground floor of one of the abandoned Coppola complex apartments next to the Catholic Church. The walls have been painted with scenes from Africa, including flowering trees, mountains and rivers. Piles of firewood, broken bottles and paper litter the concrete floor. There is a distinct smell of cat urine and dead animals.

Once I followed an African man on a bicycle as he carried a live chicken by the legs to the abandoned apartment, which is under heavy guard when the witch doctor is in. When he's not there, all that's left are remnants of his rituals, including stones around burnt areas of the concrete and paintings on the walls.

The man with the chicken was coming from a small African market run by an elderly Nigerian woman with platinum hair, whom her customers call Mamma Lucky but who introduced herself as Pamela to me the first time I went in. The tiny store smells like cardamom and pipe smoke and looks like a normal *alimentari*, or traditional Italian grocery store, with dusty boxes of pasta and tins of tomatoes on the low shelves near the front entrance.

An old-style deli case along the left wall is filled with closed plastic bags with African names scrawled on them in royal blue marker. Mamma Lucky generally sits behind an old wooden table at the back of the store that is not visible from the door. A bell tied with a red ribbon to the glass door chimes when some-one walks in, giving her plenty of warning to shuffle things around on her table if she needs to.

Nigerians can buy any number of spices and prepared foods from their home country with euro or Nigerian naira. There are postcards from Nigeria taped to one wall and a faded and torn Nigerian flag on the other.

Mamma Lucky also sells little plastic relics of African gods and live reptiles and small mice that she keeps in shoeboxes with tiny air holes near her table and which can be used for the rituals. When the bell rings, the little rodents scurry around, making scraping sounds inside the cardboard boxes.

The larger animals are kept in little cages in a small store-room in the back of the store, which has a door that opens up to the shared courtyard in the back. There is no cash register or receipt book on Mamma Lucky's desk, just a drawer where she keeps the money in neat stacks. An elderly African gentle-man who appears to be deaf often sits across from her at the worn wooden table. Sometimes others are there playing Eléwénjewé, a popular Nigerian card game that dates back to the slave-trade-era.

Mamma Lucky is friendly enough, but questions about the prostitution racket happening on the streets near the store are clearly not welcome. She says the girls are out there by choice, that they do it because "they like the sex – you know, it is very natural."

The local undercover police officer who pointed me to Mamma Lucky's store says she is a retired madam who still makes money off the racket. He says the witch doctors have often performed the curse in the back room of her shop, but since black magic is not illegal, there is nothing to be done to stop it. The cops watch her store to see who goes in and out, more to keep an eye on the status quo than to look for illegal activity.

It is no secret at all that Mamma Lucky sells relics and animals for the curse. Many of the girls who have been saved from the streets know of her store because she also sells products for women with black skin and hair, which are difficult to find in the Italian stores in Castel Volturno. I inquired once if she could help me witness someone taking the JuJu curse, but she said that there is no way to watch it without being pulled under the spell, unless I paid at least €400 to protect myself, maybe more when I got there. In fact, she said the price would vary and couldn't be set ahead of time. The police officer advised me against it, warning that they couldn't do much to protect me if I paid cash to be involved in something that could ultimately end badly. Curious as I was, I took his advice when he refused to go with me.

Women agree to take the JuJu curse because they truly believe in it. They know that they are promising fidelity, but they have no sense of the real brainwashing that awaits them. Women who swear to the curse believe they risk insanity, infertility or even death to themselves or their families if they break the bond. But none of the women who take the curse truly understand that they are really being shackled to a pimp. Most think that they are promising to be true to a generous sponsor who cares about them, not a sex trafficker ready to exploit them.

The omertà, or vow of secrecy, attached to the curse, similar to the code of secrecy invoked by the mafia, keeps women from talking about it. As all authors of propaganda know, keeping people silent will generally stop them from joining forces to revolt.

A key feature of the Nigerian sex trafficking networks is that women control women, making it a more difficult network to break because of the hold the madams have over the girls they effectively own. That may be why only women have had the most success saving them.

Princess Inyang Okokon is an exception to most of the known rules of sex trafficking. She came to Italy in 1999 on a commercial flight on the promise that she would work as a chef in a new restaurant featuring African cuisine near Turin. Like nearly all the women who come over, she thought that the woman who recruited and "sponsored" her was a Christian and a good person, not someone connected to a pimp who would exploit her. She was among the first wave of trafficked women coming to Italy, and she is amazed how many thousands have followed the same footsteps in the last twenty years, despite attempts to get the Nigerian government to do something to stop the trafficking of women out of the country.

Princess was trafficked to one of the first madams who moved from Castel Volturno to northern Italy, and she ended up in a small town called Asti, near Turin, which was emerging as a northern hub for sex trafficking in the early 2000s, catching men looking for sex while on ski holidays or in Turin on business.

She eventually escaped sexual slavery through the help of a local priest and an Italian lawyer named Alberto Mossino, who was in the process of setting up an NGO called PIAM Onlus after noticing an influx of young Nigerian women being forced into sexual slavery in the area.[28] Alberto hadn't had much luck until he met Princess, who was able to help him reach the women. On his own, he seemed too much like a client. But before she could help him she had to pay off her madam, which she did with Alberto's help.

Their mission was noble. They offered a safe house for a few women at a time who wanted to escape. Princess knew exactly what they were up against and they hired guards who would keep the madams and their henchmen from stealing back their prized sex workers.

Princess and Alberto eventually fell in love and later married in what is truly a story of trust and faith. Together they have saved more than two hundred women off the streets around Turin.[29] Now Princess and other women whom she and Alberto have saved try to go to meet the rescue boats when they arrive in the southern Italian ports to warn as many Nigerian women as they can that their sponsor is a pimp.

They have to work fast because the traffickers are waiting in the refugee camps to ferry the girls to their madams, often within the first week of their arrival. If they can convince the women to stay inside the camps or try to get them moved to safer places, they might be able to escape a life of forced sexual slavery. It is much harder to rescue them once they have met their madams.

If the young women have the name of their madam, Princess reports them to the police. But, more often, the girls are too naive and unaware to ask for a real name when they are promised a new life. The phone numbers they carry are often automatically forwarded to intermediaries or to the madams' unlisted numbers, making them impossible to trace.

Nuns and women like Princess may be able to save a handful of women from sexual slavery, but the madams are the only ones who will truly be able to break the cycle. The madams are the most secretive and least understood in the entire racket. They act as both mother and pimp, as both jailor and savior. Many are also invariably victims of trafficking themselves who have found justice only in inflicting pain on others in revenge. Madams are women who were conditioned or bribed or coerced or somehow convinced to inflict the same horrendous pain they suffered on younger women. They are often still exploited, just now by higher-level criminals.

In 2012, a woman in her late forties known to be a madam was murdered and left to bleed to death on the beach in the old

Coppola Village. She was naked and showed signs of sexual violence. She had cigarette burns on her thighs and vagina and she had torture injuries from the tip of a knife around her breasts and neck. According to the autopsy, she also had old scars where bits of her skin had been removed, likely from her own experience with the JuJu.

She bled to death from a wound to her neck that paralyzed her but did not kill her instantly. Her death was not mourned in Castel Volturno, but it caught the attention of police who could not identify signs of Camorra involvement. In the end, even though she was a madam known to police, she was also an undocumented migrant and finding justice for her death was not a priority. She is buried in the cemetery in Pozzuoli, in a section paid for by the state and designated for missing persons and those without families.

Police rarely chase madams, but in 2016, the anti-Mafia division of the state police (known as the DDA) conducted an operation called "Skin Trade" that uncovered one of the networks set up to get women out of the CARA Mineo camp and onto the streets.[30] Among those arrested were Tina Nosakhare, twenty-eight, Faby Osagie Idehen, twenty-three and Cynthia Samuel, twenty-four, who worked with what were termed "connection men" inside the Mineo camp.

Also arrested were several women thought to be madams in and around Castel Volturno, including Gift Akoro, twenty-eight, who called herself Madam Pamela, and Toyin Lokiki, thirty-one, who called herself Madam Juliet. Among their possessions were relics and powders attached to the JuJu curse.

For me, the most interesting arrest was that of a woman called Irene Ebhoadaghe, forty-four, who called herself Mummy Shade, who was waiting for three young women who had arrived at Mineo in 2016, one of whom was Joy, the young woman whom I had met outside the CARA Mineo camp a month earlier.[31] Joy was named specifically in the arrest warrant as a victim of trafficking even though, at the time we met, she had no idea that was her fate. She was given asylum and moved to northern Europe to join a relative after cooperating with the police.

I learned later that an undercover police officer who had been tipped off by one of the aid agencies working inside CARA Mineo had eventually picked her up on the road leading through the citrus groves and convinced her to help them catch the people who had trafficked her. Without her cooperation, the "Skin Trade" arrests would have likely never happened.

I caught up with her by email thanks to a local anti-trafficking advocate in Sicily who took an interest in her case and acted as a liaison with the court. She remembered our conversation outside CARA Mineo and she wrote back that she had been a fool.

"I was so stupid," she wrote in her first email. "How could I have been so trusting? How could I have been so dumb?"

I wrote back to console her, telling her not to worry, that many women fell into the same trap.

She wrote again. "You knew about this. Why didn't you tell me what was going to happen?"

I had tried, I thought, but obviously not hard enough.

"I asked you if you knew about the girls like you who had to be prostitutes," I wrote in a feeble response, and then I admitted that I hadn't known exactly what to do, that I didn't want to cross the "ethical boundaries" of journalism. In fact, I was more concerned that I might be wrong or that, even if I was right, I had no idea how to help her. I was also selfishly scared that if I intervened, I might get caught up in some sort of retaliation act, that someone might harm me or my children for taking one of the madam's precious "assets" off the streets.

She wrote back a third and final time. "You could have saved me."

And she's right. I should have, no matter what journalistic ethics or fear I thought were guiding me. But, like everyone else, I just turned away. I wrote back and said I was sorry. I never heard from her again despite countless attempts to reach her.

The "Skin Trade" operation that, thanks to Joy, netted arrests is a rare success. More often, the madams are not a priority and not on the most wanted lists, not least of all because they use false names. In many cases, they are well known to local authorities but they have been able to convince them to protect them, often through the gift of sex. They are masters at evoking fear from the black magic JuJu curse from the women they own, which is the primary reason Nigerian women do not leave the sex trafficking racket.

Superstition and witchcraft are a well-documented part of the Nigerian culture. In 2016, a toddler named Hope from the wealthy, oil-rich southern state of Akwa Ibom in Nigeria made headlines across the world when his family rejected him because they thought he was a witch.[32] They left him to die on the streets of Uyo until Danish aid worker Anja Lovén, who runs the African Children's Aid Education and Development Foundation orphanage for children who are thought to be witches, saved him from death. She was able to raise over a million dollars for his medical bills, which included surgery from birth defects and the drastic effect of malnutrition on his internal organs.

Not all the women who undergo the JuJu ritual in Nigeria are destined for sex trafficking abroad. Many fathers and husbands subject their daughters and wives to the curse as part of a culture of obedience in Nigeria. Others volunteer to take it to ward off bad luck or infertility. Rituals have long been used in Edo state as a form of manipulation between men and women in marriages and between parents and children in families, but in the 1980s, black magic priests in Nigeria started working more commonly with human traffickers and extended the reach of the curse.[33]

The curse is a daunting obstacle for those who try to save women from sexual slavery. The nuns, like all devout Catholics, are well equipped with spiritual tools to fight off the devil, but they have had to tailor the standard Catholic teachings against evil to ward off specific JuJu magic in their struggle for the souls of the Nigerian victims of trafficking. The sisters must not only convince the women that they will be safe if they leave their madams, they must also convince them that the JuJu curse won't follow them.

One of the reasons the Catholic nuns have had success getting women to stay off the streets is easily due to the nuns' familiarity with fighting evil. Many of the women who are trafficked are Christian, so they can be helped with the Bible. But most aren't Catholic, which does create an obstacle since nuns are trained in the Catholic catechism. The nuns often ask the women to pray for salvation against the curse, but letting go of the fear that their madams will come back for them, or that they will be killed, is almost impossible, which is why so many still feel they must pay off their bogus debts even after they are saved.

Even after they escape the street, the hardest part is trying to convince the woman that the curse won't follow them. Father Hyginus Obia is a Nigerian Catholic priest at the Santa Maria del Monte Verginella church near the main train station in Naples.

The church's delicate white facade seems out of place between two oppressive ochre colored apartment blocks. Even the square bell tower looks as if it has been stuffed between the buildings, jutted up against someone's apartment, as if no one knew where else to put it.

During the week, the narrow street in front of the church is lined with tables where vendors sell trinkets, household goods, second hand books and "Made in China" plastic toys under faded umbrellas. On Sundays, the tables give way to badly parked cars and scooters.

The church is known locally as the "ethnic" or "black" church because most of the parishioners are African. On a blisteringly hot Sunday morning in July 2016, I sat in on one of the masses. The men wore suits and the women wore colorful

African dresses with matching headdresses. Despite the stifling heat and lack of air conditioning, the church was full and the mass lasted well over an hour. Afterwards, everyone went up to the altar for a group picture with Father Obia. I went back several months later and the same thing happened, including the photo shoot at the end. It was as if just surviving another week was enough reason to celebrate and commemorate the event.

On my second visit, after the photo session was finished and everyone had shaken hands and thanked Father Obia, he told me that there aren't many Nigerian women in the parish. They are hard to convince to come, he says. Even those who have escaped sex slavery feel embarrassed and looked down upon by the other Africans who attend mass. Most of the parishioners are from Ghana and former Italian colonies Ethiopia and Eritrea. Father Obia is from Nigeria. He trained in Belgium and Rome before coming to Naples. He works together with Father Tonino Palmese, the local priest in charge of Neapolitan charities for the diocese and an ardent anti-Mafia champion for the local community.

Together with the nuns, the priests have called on a local Catholic exorcist named Father Giuseppe Scarpitta who performs exorcisms between 9 A.M. and noon and 4:30 to 8:30 P.M. on Tuesdays and by special appointment. All exorcists trained by the Catholic Church perform rituals against soul possession by a variety of evil spirits, including black magic and JuJu curses. But in Naples, Father Scarpitta and the other exorcists have learned to personalize the ceremony to include items not normally found in Catholic exorcism rites.

It must be noted that the rite of exorcism is incredibly common in the Roman Catholic Church, especially in southern Italy. In a typical month, local exorcists can perform more than two hundred exorcisms. It is not uncommon to witness the rite. In 2015, there was such concern for the spiritual health of the nearby community of Castellammare di Stabia after a spate of religious artifact thefts and damage to crosses, that the local parish rented a helicopter and performed an exorcism rite from the sky over the entire community.[34]

Not only were the locals convinced their souls had been saved, but some twenty-eight blocked fountains from the local ancient baths suddenly sprang back to life after years without water. It was a miracle, according to townspeople.

When possible, the Neapolitan exorcists try to mimic the JuJu rite by including vials of powders or liquids to represent the same elements of the original curse. They follow the Catholic exorcism rite to the letter, but the enhancements work to convince the girls that they are not just exorcising a demon but also reversing the curse. The only other way is to return to the original witch doctor.

Exorcisms can be performed in private homes, but the one I witnessed was carried out in the very creepy basement of the La Chiesa della Missione ai Vergine, or Church of the Mission of the Virgins, on Via Vergini near the archeological museum in the center of Naples. The church, built in 1724 by the Neapolitan architect Luigi Vanvitelli, has a baroque facade and unassuming interior. Absent are the colorful frescoes and ceiling adornments for which many Neapolitan churches are known. Like the African church, it is lodged between two buildings that appear to have been built around it, likely illegally.

I attended an exorcism for a Nigerian woman I will call May, who was receiving mental health care after being systematically tortured by a client in Naples who kept her tied to a bed in his apartment for several months. She looked vacant and traumatized. She was accompanied by Sister Maria Teresa, who had urged her at least to try the exorcism to rid herself of the curse since the mental health treatment wasn't helping and certainly didn't address breaking the curse.

Back in the basement of the Church of the Mission of the Virgins, Father Scarpitta laid out the altar with a pewter aspergillum to sprinkle holy water, an elaborate crucifix and his well-worn prayer book. May knelt on a small kneeler with tattered green velvet in front of him. Sister Maria Teresa stood behind her with her hand firmly on May's shoulder, as if to hold her down in case she started to levitate. The only smell was that of old candle wax from the hundreds of used votive candles stacked up in a corner of the basement that had been lit by the little old ladies and widows of Naples to honor their dead.

The exorcism rite is hardly like it is depicted in pop culture, with the exception of the dark church basement. According to the Catholic Church Book of Rites, the exorcist must first go to confession to clear his own soul, thereby not offering any competition in the way of an unclean soul for the devil during the ritual.[35] I did not witness Father Scarpitta's confession, but I assume he followed the protocol.

Then, wearing a purple stole over a simple tunic, he sprinkled holy water on himself, May and Sister Maria Teresa before starting a long list of prayers including the litany of the saints. Twenty minutes later, he cast out the devil, reciting a prayer in Latin that translates to the one listed in the Roman Catholic catechism.

"I cast you out, unclean spirit, along with every Satanic power of the enemy, every specter from hell, and all your fell companions; in the name of our Lord Jesus Christ," he said in Latin, forming the sign of the cross first on him and then towards May, whose head was down.

> Be gone and stay far from this creature of God. For it is He who commands you, He who flung you headlong from the heights of heaven into the depths of hell. It is He who commands you, He who once stilled the sea and the wind and the storm. Hearken, therefore, and tremble in fear, Satan, you enemy of the faith, you foe of the human race, you begetter of death, you robber of life, you corrupter of justice, you root of all evil and vice; seducer of men, betrayer of the nations, instigator of

envy, font of avarice, fomenter of discord, author of pain and sorrow.

May didn't move during the entire rite, although Sister Maria Teresa shifted somewhat nervously from foot to foot. I was one of about a dozen people kneeling in the pews behind them. Being raised as a Catholic myself, it is very difficult not to kneel when others kneel. We all watched intently. I was half waiting for smoke to come out of her body or some other incredible spectacle to unfold. It didn't, but when it was over May couldn't keep her eyes open. She wanted to lie down in the pews and go to sleep. Sister Maria Teresa helped her up the stairs to the main floor of the church where she tried to lie down again. They got into a dark blue Fiat Panda double parked outside with another nun waiting behind the wheel and sped away. I have no idea what happened to her. Father Scarpitta holds weekly prayer services as post-exorcism spiritual maintenance to keep the bad spirits away from the souls he has cleared of the devil.

When I posed the question about exorcising the JuJu curse to Cardinal Nichols, who, as an Englishman, I had expected to raise an eyebrow, he said, "why not?"

As he explained it, Satan is not a one-size-fits-all, and skilled exorcists are trained to understand the particular spiritual weakness with which they are faced. If a devout woman believes it is the JuJu curse that has possessed her soul, there is nothing in the Catholic rulebook that would stop an exorcist from addressing that particular demon, so long as he follows the rite. "If it works to free them, then what is the problem?" he asked.

The Catholic cemetery in Pozzallo, Sicily, is home
to the ornate tombs of Mafia dons and the nameless
graves of unknown migrants and refugees.

4

ITALY'S DNA: GOD, GIRLS AND THE MAFIA

"Having black skin in this country is a limit to a civil life. Racism is here too: it is made of arrogance, the abuse of power, and daily violence towards those who ask for none other than solidarity and respect . . . Sooner or later one of us will be killed, and then you will know that we exist."
– Jerry Essan Masslo, South African migrant murdered near Naples

BAIA VERDE – In 1955, around the time the Coppola brothers were drawing up plans to create their utopian village off the coast near Castel Volturno, Pupetta Maresca committed her first murder. She was twenty years old and heavily pregnant at the time. The former beauty queen was on her way to the cemetery near Casal di Principe to lay flowers on her dead Mafioso husband's tomb, which she had done every day since his murder a few months earlier, when she saw her husband's killer on the street. She ordered her driver to stop, got out of the car and shot her husband's killer dead with the Smith & Wesson .38 pistol she had retrieved from her husband's nightstand, and which she carried in her handbag for just such an occasion. The killing avenged the murder of her husband, whose death had been ordered by the rival Camorra clansman. She was quickly caught and tried for the crime, for which she had no remorse, telling the judge she would do it again without a thought. From that point on, she was known as "Madame Camorra" or "the Diva of Crime," and she set the bar when it came to the level of loyalty expected by a Camorra woman to her man.

Pupetta's son was born in prison where he stayed with her behind bars for the first three years of his life before being handed over to his maternal grandmother. When Pupetta was released at the age of thirty-one, she fell in love with another gangster with whom she had twins. A jealous man, he would later be accused of killing her first son, whose body has never been found but which is believed to be buried in the cement pillar of an overpass near Naples. She stayed with her son's suspected killer anyway out of loyalty – a loyalty she had created but from which she was ultimately unable to escape. Pupetta was eventually pardoned even though she was implicated in a string of murders and other Camorra crimes. She retired to a terraced apartment in Sorrento where she still lives alone at the time of writing.

Far from being scorned because of her criminal ways, Pupetta Maresca has enjoyed considerable fame. Songs have been written about her and when she was on trial for murder, she received dozens of marriage proposals. She was the inspiration for the protagonist of the 1958 film *La Sfida* (*The Heat*) as well as the subject of a made-for-TV movie called *The Case of Pupetta Maresca*, in which she was played by Alessandra Mussolini, the granddaughter of the dictator Benito Mussolini.

Not surprisingly perhaps, Pupetta owned one of the original villas in Castel Volturno on the Baia Verde near the Coppola Village. It was there that she spent many summer weekends, hosting parties for Camorra associates and occasionally harboring fugitives. The house was also allegedly used as a drug warehouse in later years and was confiscated around the time the first Coppola Village towers were brought down.

In 2010, the Italian state gave Pupetta's villa to a migrant rights advocacy group known as the Jerry Essan Masslo Association. Masslo was a black South African who was murdered in Italy in 1989 in a violent racist hate crime at the hands of the Camorra after he stood up against the slave labor conditions he and other refugees were forced to endure. He and scores of other Africans worked for a few lire a day and had to sleep in appalling labor camps with little attention to nutrition or hygiene. He was part of the original surge of African laborers who came to work in the tomato fields long before the Camorra poisoned the land or the area became a hotbed for sexual slavery. Masslo was given a state funeral and his death sparked protests against racism in what was then (and very much still is) a monoculture Italy.

Two days before he was murdered, he was interviewed by a journalist working on the program *Non Solo Nero* (*Not Just Black*) for RAI's TG2 news program. His quote proved prophetic. "I thought that in Italy I would find a space to live, a breath of civilization, and a reception that would allow me to live in peace and to cultivate the dream of a future without barriers or prejudices," he said. "But I am disappointed. Having black skin in this country is a limit to a civil life. Racism is here too: it is made of arrogance, the abuse of power, and daily violence towards those who ask for none other than solidarity and respect. We in the Third World are contributing to the development of your country, but it seems that this has no weight. Sooner or later one of us will be killed, and then you will know that we exist."[36]

He didn't know that it would be him. The association that bears his name continues to fight racism and maltreatment of asylum seekers when and where it can. They sponsor a group called Other Horizons, which turned Pupetta's villa into a tailor shop called Casa di Alice (House of Alice) where Italian and African women work together to create "Made in Castel

Volturno" clothing with Italian-inspired designs and African fabrics. The tailor shop is also an homage to those killed at the Ob Ob Exotic Fashions tailor shop in 2008, which is discussed in the next chapter.

Each summer, the House of Alice holds fashion shows in Pupetta's sculpted garden, where gangsters once plotted and celebrated their crimes. Occasionally, Nigerian women who have been rescued from sexual slavery work as models in the show. The house has been stripped of Madame Camorra's personal decor, but the initials that she had inlaid in gold leaf into the fireplace's mantelpiece were left intact. A plaque now hangs on that fireplace that says, "The Camorra lost here."

Similar plaques adorn a number of buildings in and around the Land of Fires that have been confiscated from the Camorra and handed over to those with better intentions. There are former dairy shops that now produce "mafia-free" buffalo mozzarella and a handful of other legitimate businesses trying to find their footing in an area that has only ever been known for criminality.

Still, despite the sporadic successes in the battle against organized crime, it would be a stretch to say the Camorra, or any of the other crime syndicates, is losing influence and power in Italy. If anything, their power seems to be growing, now stretching much further north. In many ways, Italy's Mafia organizations define this country. Prime ministers and judges have been extinguished for standing up to them as often as they have been brought down for colluding with them.

Inherent corruption, the by-product of a country under the influence of organized crime for decades, is in many ways the fabric of Italian society. It exists in public school playgrounds and multi-national boardrooms in equal measure. I will never forget the day that my son came home from his Italian preschool class asking for pocket change because he had "to pay the boss for permission to play with them" because he was a blue-eyed foreigner.

"Why?" I asked.

"It's just the rule, mom." I sent the money and only told the administrator about the incident after he had moved on to an international school in first grade. I didn't want to risk his happiness over some loose change.

The longer one lives in this country, the more understandable the corruption is. Why do something the correct way, which often consists of wading through thick layers of bureaucracy, when there is always someone offering a shortcut for a small fee? I paid a woman on a scooter the equivalent of $50 to get my fiscal code. The process of getting the paperwork in order would have taken me days. She was back in a few hours, having taken some back door. No doubt the $50 I gave her went to whomever she bribed to get my document fast. I also know a man who will take all of my parking tickets and "make them go away" for a small fee, never mind that I got them fairly or that the money should go to help improve the roads. The idea that getting away with a shortcut is somehow a victory is, of course, why inefficiency reigns and why Italians need to cut corners in the first place. If one generation just did things by the rule of law, it might stop the cycle, but no one teaches that right is better than wrong, primarily because it's so much harder to do it the right way.

Transparency International's Corruption Perception Index consistently puts Italy at or near the top of the list of the most corrupt countries in Europe and often in a dead heat with Cuba in the global ranking.[37]

Complacency, which has allowed widespread corruption to persist, has nearly ruined the country. People who don't pay taxes tend to justify it by saying the government is corrupt. But the government is also corrupt because people don't pay taxes. In 2017, the state-run debt collection agency that collects taxes and fines was closed down because it was charging inordinate late fees and making massive profits. Even Google settled a tax dispute, agreeing to pay Italy €306 million for skirting the law and not paying tax on its revenues in the country.[38] Two years earlier, Apple had to pay €318 million under similar circumstances.[39] When in Rome, as they say.

The labor laws are such that it is often impossible to fire people, so no one gets full-time jobs. Those who do often don't even go to work because they can't be fired. There are exceptions, of course, and successful businesses that do play by the rules. But there are literally hundreds of stories about people who are paid under the table to punch timecards for those who have never even been to their workstations while those who are paid under the table are the ones doing the work. As Prime Minister, Silvio Berlusconi once cited the black economy (that exists outside of taxation) as an important part of Italy's overall GDP, essentially endorsing the continuation of the practice of not paying income tax. The exploitation of young workers, women and the law are as common as pasta.

Every time there is an earthquake or a flood, corruption is painfully apparent, especially in the construction sector, where building regulations are frequently ignored. When a devastating earthquake hit the city of L'Aquila in 2009, killing more than three hundred people, the streets were covered with piles of beach sand that had been used to mix the cement, instead of the more expensive special gravel that is required. When an earthquake hit the Emilia-Romagna area in 2012, Italy's chief anti-Mafia prosecutor Franco Roberti warned that the Mafia was waiting in the wings to exploit rebuilding efforts. "Post-earthquake reconstruction is historically a delicious morsel for criminal groups and business interests," he said. Despite this, nothing was really done to ensure that bids weren't fixed or that Mafia-related businesses weren't benefitting.

When another devastating earthquake hit the central Italian region near the town of Amatrice in 2016, a public school that had just been renovated with anti-seismic reinforcements collapsed. Upon further investigation, it was determined that the compliance certificate for the anti-seismic upgrade had been forged. The earthquake struck in the middle of the night during the summer break, but whoever forged that document clearly had no way of knowing an earthquake wouldn't strike during a busy school day. Nobody cared. So far, no one has even been charged for the forgery that put the lives of hundreds of children at risk.

In 2014, the discovery of Rome's so-called Mafia Capitale that apparently ran the capital's municipal government for many years sent shockwaves across Italy. For months after, Rome's city services fell apart. Without the Mafia in charge, no one seemed to know where to start to legitimize the city contracts. At least the Mafia had shell companies that collected garbage, swept the streets and cleaned the gutters as a cover for their fake contracts. The vacuum created when the mob was cleaned out brought the city to its knees.[40]

The Mafia Capitale had also infiltrated the asylum seeker centers across the country. During the investigation that led to the group members' arrests, the alleged boss, Salvatore Buzzi, was caught on a wiretap bragging about how much money he made off the backs of the asylum seekers. "Do you have any idea how much I earn on immigrants?" he was heard telling an associate. "Drugs are less profitable." Buzzi and his associates were sentenced to decades in prison in a trial that ended in 2017, though Italy's system allows for automatic appeals so the gangsters could serve very little time.

The Roman mobsters who made a financial killing in the exploitation of asylum seekers were tied to a scam where they allegedly bought migrants' names from CARA Mineo in Sicily. By law, any registered center that cares for refugees and migrants receives €35 a day per person from the state. Of that sum, €2.50 is earmarked to go directly to the asylum seeker so he or she can save money and buy essentials that are not provided. Among the many ways the organized crime syndicates exploit this system is by colluding with small refugee centers who register migrants who are actually still staying inside larger centers like CARA Mineo or who have disappeared altogether.

The administrators of the larger centers get a kickback for selling the personal details of the asylum seekers, and the smaller centers pocket the daily allowances. Everyone wins, except of course the migrants and refugees. This is one of the primary ways trafficked women can leave so easily. Even if they are no longer at the centers, their names tend to stay on the lists, which benefits the centers as the money they receive to care for them can be put to other purposes. Those who suffer the most are of course the legitimate refugees who then end up living in over-crowded centers, which take on more migrants to earn revenue even though they have only emptied their beds on paper. If the system worked as it was designed, trafficked women who disappear might have a better chance at being rescued because their absence would cause concern. In the current situation, it causes merely a sense of relief.

The phenomenon of bilking the asylum system is not limited to Rome. In 2017, anti-Mafia police arrested sixty-eight people, including the local parish priest, in the Calabrian town of Isola di Capo Rizzuto, where one of the country's largest migrant and refugee reception centers has been in operation for more than a decade. Investigators say that the criminals siphoned off tens of millions of euros in public funds that were intended to better the lives of the asylum seekers while they waited for their applications to be heard. General Giuseppe Governale, the local chief of the anti-Mafia forces, said the center was effectively an ATM for the 'Ndrangheta Mafia. Nicola Gratteri, the prosecutor in charge of the investigation, said detectives filmed the appalling conditions inside the center. "There was never enough food and we even filmed the quality of food," he said. "It was the kind of food we usually give to the pigs." The group set up shell companies that were being paid to provide food services, but instead the money was used to buy apartments, land, cars and yachts.[41]

The fact that new criminal groups and organized scams continue to emerge certainly seems to suggest that Italy's criminal DNA is still as strong as ever. In addition to the new Mafia Capitale in Rome, members of Italy's historic organized crime syndicates continue to be among the most powerful people in the country. They are in government. They are in businesses. They are like cockroaches – one might get caught, but you know there are hundreds more lurking in the shadows ready to take their place.

The Sicilian Mafia (or Cosa Nostra), the Calabria 'Ndrangheta and the Neapolitan Camorra are forever expanding and adjusting their business models based on current trends. There are criminal groups in the southern region of Puglia (the heel of Italy's boot) as well, but the notorious Sacra Corona Unita lost power in the early 2000s after the cigarette and drug smuggling channels across the Adriatic from the Balkan states were shut down. It is a unique success story in Italy's eternal and infernal fight against organized crime, aided in part by a successful clampdown on illegal smuggling on the Balkan side of the Adriatic Sea. Still, many more smaller groups are on the rise in Puglia, taking advantage of any number of opportunities to exploit and prosper. During the summer of 2017, four people were murdered in a vendetta shooting on a lonely highway in Puglia, which was a stark reminder that the criminal gangs are still present in the territory. In fact, anti-Mafia chief Franco Roberti said that there had been three hundred murders in Puglia in the last three decades, eighty percent of which remain unsolved, the killers never brought to justice.

The death sentence imposed on Saviano for exposing the Camorra's crime activity to the outside world has done little to stop him. His other book, *ZeroZeroZero*, about the illicit cocaine trade named after the high quality of the Camorra's powder, was also widely acclaimed for its cutting-edge investigative work.

The first time I interviewed Saviano was in 2007, after his first book, *Gomorrah*, had been made into a movie. We met on a rainy morning in the palatial Villa Borghese park in Rome. The whole death threat and armed police escort routine was new to him. He held an oversized black umbrella and I took notes. It wasn't an ideal interview situation, but he hadn't been for a walk in a park for some time by then and relished the opportunity to be outside. I, on the other hand, was terrified someone might hit me when they tried to shoot him. I kept looking back at the police escort walking about fifty feet behind us and tried to slow down our pace.

The second time I interviewed him, maybe a year later, was at Mondadori Publishing offices near the American embassy in Rome. We sat in front of large glass window in one of their fancy meeting rooms, and I took diligent notes while waiting for the sound of glass to break from a gunshot. Saviano's calm demeanor and devil-may-care attitude towards the threats against him invites paranoia.

By the time of our third interview, two years after that, reality had sunk in for the muckraker. We drove around in the car driven by his armed guards who told lewd jokes and smoked cigarettes in the front seat. By then, he couldn't be bothered to take any risks for an interview just to show his bravado. It suited me just fine. Now he has become somewhat of a celebrity and doesn't give so many interviews. Instead, he writes splashy columns for *La Repubblica* newspaper and presents big-think events on television when he's not going viral with pithy comments and tweets.

What has struck me about Saviano through the years is how connected he remains to the same sources who helped him report *Gomorrah* – proof, perhaps, that he truly is of the Land of Fires. That world is part of his DNA in ways that are at once alarming and immeasurable. Despite the fact that he is really living in what amounts to a prison, I wouldn't be surprised if he was often back there, working undercover, interviewing clansmen and cops just like he did in the beginning.

Saviano is especially versed in the role of women and the Camorra. As he has written many times, Camorra women are not at all like those depicted in pop culture. Their role has evolved, forever changed from "that of a maternal figure and helper in times of misfortune to a serious manager who concerns herself almost exclusively with the business and financial end of things, delegating the fighting and illegal trafficking to others."

This enhanced role for women within organized crime is light years ahead of Italian society, where only twenty-six percent of women work in professional positions and few ever reach managerial roles. The World Economic Forum's Gender Gap Index consistently points out how behind Italy is on wage parity and equal opportunity, which doesn't seem to extend to the underworld. There is no room whatsoever, though, for foreign women in organized crime. In Calabria, 'Ndrangheta men are only allowed to have foreign women as mistresses. If they marry, it must be to an Italian, preferably one from Calabria.

Women involved in the Mafia can be found in courtrooms and prisons alongside men across the country. It wasn't always that way, of course. In her 1997 book *Mafia Women*, Clare Longrigg points out that for many years, women involved in organized crime got a pass when it came to legal repercussions. She points to a 1983 court ruling in Palermo, in which a woman accused of money laundering was acquitted for the reason that "women could not be guilty of money-laundering because they are not autonomous and are anyway too stupid to take part in the difficult world of business."

The Camorra may have evolved since then, but clearly not all women are yet on equal footing. Wives are often told less than mistresses, daughters sometimes trusted more than mothers. One thing, however, is sure: the "code of ethics" that guided even the most cold-hearted criminals not to kill women and children has all but disappeared. Now, they can be targeted just as much as men.

In 2014, a three-year-old boy named Domenico was shot in the head along with his mother and her lover because she had turned state's evidence after someone killed her Mafioso husband. The murder made headlines for the sheer audacity of the crime, but it suggested a larger trend. "These men of honor used to forbid the killing of priests, women and children," Giacomo Di Gennaro, a Neapolitan sociologist specializing in organized crime, told Agence France-Presse at the time.[42] "Their control over the territory was so strong that it was not necessary." Today, the boundaries of territories change so quickly, all lines are crossed. That includes the treatment of sex-trafficked women, who are considered less than human.

Italy's organized crime groups and Mafia also have a somewhat complicated relationship with the Catholic Church. Camorra men tend to be uncomfortable with Catholic nuns, especially those like Sister Rita who are not at all afraid to stand up to them. In fact, all Italian men have a funny habit of grabbing their crotches when they see a nun, apparently to ward off bad luck. Due to their association with hospitals and cemeteries, they are considered a bad omen.

While some people living in and around Naples are reluctant to file a complaint with the police against a member of the Camorra out of fear of retaliation, Sister Rita regularly marches into her local precinct to name clan members whom she knows to be colluding with the Nigerian gangs. She is also quick to recount the well-documented reports about police across Italy who force the girls to have sex for free in exchange for a pass if their documents aren't in order. Sister Rita denounced a police officer who she says took advantage of one of the women who had escaped to Casa Ruth. According to the police report, among the many lewd acts he forced upon her were sodomy with his Billy club and making her lick the semen off his badge after he had ejaculated upon it. He was eventually detained but charges were dropped after the woman returned to Nigeria and couldn't testify against him. He was removed from his post in the Land of Fires but is still a police officer in northern Italy.

In late 2015, three officers in Caserta (Alessandro Albano, a superintendent with the force, forty-eight; Domenico Petrillo, forty-one; and Nunziante Camarca, thirty-seven) were arrested for having sex with Nigerian girls who had come to them for help getting out of the racket. The alleged sex took place inside the police station. The men are also accused of having sex with other girls in Castel Volturno in squad cars and armored vehicles.

Not only did they not help the women escape, the women say the cops refused to pay them for sex, putting them at great risk with their madams for not earning enough even though the general rule on the Domitiana is that police don't have to pay. The trio also allegedly delivered large orders of cocaine for one of the Camorra clans using patrol cars. When the men were arrested, Camarca had several checks worth around $3,000 in his possession, potentially to be recycled back to the Camorra. The police are currently facing charges for Mafia collusion, but none for further exploiting the sex-trafficked women.

However, beyond the shelter's cars being stolen and the odd sophomoric acts of vandalism, the Camorra has not directly threatened the nuns at Casa Ruth. Whether it is out of respect or fear of "God's wrath" is unclear.

I found my own car tires flattened after one of my many visits to Casa Ruth, all four punctured by something sharp. When I went to the local police and, after explaining that I was working on a project about sex trafficking, asked whether I should report the incident as a crime or a threat, they laughed at me, as if I should be lucky it was only the tires that had been slashed.

Sister Rita is undeterred. "They aren't going to kill a nun," she jokes. "They know I am not a real threat, and that I can never save all these girls. They know they will win in the end."

Until recently, the Church often turned a blind eye to Mafia crimes. Mafiosi were married and buried in some of the most beautiful churches in Italy, and even in Rome there are known mobsters interred in marble tombs next to cardinals and popes.

One of the most famous examples can be found in the basilica of Saint Apollinare, an Opus Dei church on the Piazza Navona in Italy's capital. In 2012, Italian investigators pried open the tomb of Enrico "Renatino" De Pedis, a prominent member of the infamous Magliana organized-crime gang that has since dismantled. Renatino had been ambushed and murdered by rival gang members in 1990. Investigators were hoping they might find the body of fifteen-year-old Emanuela Orlandi, thought to be interred with him.

Orlandi was the daughter of a mid-level Vatican employee who disappeared in June 1983 after leaving her parents' Vatican apartment for a music lesson in a school adjacent to the Sant'Apollinare church. She was last seen getting into a dark green BMW and her disappearance has been one of great embarrassment for the Church and a delight for conspiracy theorists, some of whom say she is being kept as a sex slave in a monastery somewhere in the country. Her body wasn't buried with the mobster, but the fact that he was in a marble tomb in an important Roman Church raised eyebrows in certain circles and nods of understanding and complacency in others.

It's certainly not the last time the Church was accused of complicity in criminal activity. During the height of the 2015 summer season in Rome, the powerful Casamonica family, with criminal ties to both the Camorra and the 'Ndrangheta, was able to pull off a spectacular stunt that showed that organized crime is alive and well.[43] Authorities say the family rakes in an annual income of around $40 million in illegal activities, like loan sharking, racketeering and extortion, and wields considerable power in Rome.

When Vittorio, one of the patriarchs of the family, succumbed to cancer, he was given the kind of send-off generally associated with a respected city leader – what amounted to a state funeral with all the trimmings – a helicopter dropped rose petals from the sky and six black stallions pulled a gilded glass carriage carrying the mobster's ornate coffin through the streets of Rome to the San Giovanni Bosco church in a Roman suburb that bears the Casamonica name. Police stopped traffic to let the procession pass.

Theme music from *The Godfather* and *2001: A Space Odyssey* blared as the funeral procession passed. Giant banners were draped across the church facade with photos of the mafia don dressed in white, a giant bedazzled cross hanging from his neck as he hovered over a shot of the Roman Colosseum. One said: "King of Rome;" another: "You've conquered Rome, now you'll conquer paradise." The mayor and city councilors were all away for their summer holidays but quickly returned after the funeral drew consternation from the press. Only then did they question just how a known criminal could garner such respect.

Father Giancarlo Manieri, the priest and apparent close friend of the Casamonica family who officiated the funeral inside the Catholic Church, scoffed at the scandal, insisting that it was just a "normal" funeral. In actuality, it was a blatant and embarrassing slap in the face for Italy's capital by a notorious crime family.

There are international cases of the Church's complicity, too. In 1982, an Italian banker named Roberto Calvi was found hanging under Blackfriars Bridge on the edge of London's financial district with bricks and $15,000 in three different currencies in his pockets. He had earned the nick-name "God's Banker" while running Banco Ambrosiano, a major shareholder in the Vatican Bank. When Banco Ambrosiano collapsed, he was investigated and charged with white-collar crimes of mismanagement and currency manipu-lation, after which he fled to London on a private jet to await his final trial. His family attributed his death to the Corleone family of the Sicilian Cosa Nostra Mafia, which was allegedly laundering money through the Banco Ambrosiano and accounts within the Vatican's own bank. Officially, his death remains a mystery.

Bernardo Provenzano, the boss of all bosses in the Sicilian Mafia, was arrested in 2006 after forty-three years of living on the lam like a pauper. He was discovered in a tiny outbuilding on a dairy farm outside Corleone, after authorities traced his wife taking folded shirts and clean underwear to the farm. He was found with five Bibles, which authorities first thought spoke to his devout faith, which is especially common among Sicilian mobsters. When he asked for the Bibles in his prison cell, however, they grew suspicious. After further examination, they discovered that he had created an intricate system of codes based on Bible verses that he had noted in the margins of the holy books, which he wrote on tiny pieces of paper his minions folded up and carried between toes or other locations on the body to communicate with his underlings. Stumped, Italian anti-Mafia authorities sent the Bible codes – 164 in total – to the FBI to help decipher them, though at the time of writing no one has yet broken the Provenzano code. He died in prison in 2016 and was cremated and buried in the family tomb in Corleone, without a Catholic funeral, under orders of the local anti-Mafia police.

Provenzano, like other Mafiosi, used his faith to his advan-tage, relying on Catholic rituals such as confession to maintain his sense of spirituality, or perhaps to convince himself that the evil work he was doing was actually for the good of the people and, therefore, the Christian thing to do. Many mobsters are financial patrons of dioceses and even hospitals and schools run by the Catholic Church, which is as good a way as any to stay in its good graces. It is common in small towns across southern Italy for religious processions, especially at Easter, to pass by local Mafia bosses' homes to pay homage to them. Sometimes, the nod of respect is given because the local priests and Mafia dons are long-time friends; other times, it is simply because they are afraid not to. It is also a widely held belief that the Camorra drug makers cut their bricks of hashish thirty-three times (thought to be Jesus's age when he was crucified) and baptize their cocaine packets with holy water in the hope that they won't kill anyone. Pope Francis urged local parishes to deviate Easter processions from mobsters' houses in 2015, though there were reports that many small town parishes in the heart of Camorra and 'Ndrangheta country ignored the order.

In the past, those priests who did stand up to organized crime paid the ultimate price. In 1994, Camorra thugs killed Giuseppe Diana, known as Father Peppino, with two bullets to his head at his church in Casal di Principe as he prepared for mass. Father Peppino had crossed a line, essentially questioning how the various bosses could claim to be devout Catholics when they were killing members of the local communities. He had set up a center for African migrants to try to save them from working for the Camorra, and he had testified in criminal trials against clan members.

In *Gomorrah*, Saviano, who grew up in Casal di Principe, described the power struggle that led to Father Peppino's brutal murder. "In the land of the Camorra, the Christian message is not considered contradictory to Camorra activities: if the clan acts for the good of all its affiliates, the organization is seen as respecting and pursuing the Christian good," he wrote.

Religion is a constant point of reference for the Camorra, not merely as a propitiatory gesture of a cultural relic, but a spiritual force that determines the most intimate decisions. Camorra families, especially the most charismatic bosses, often consider their own actions as Calvary, their own conscience bearing the pain and weight of sin for the well-being of the group and men they rule.

Pope Francis has been the most vocal pontiff to speak out against organized crime members personally, decreeing that they are excommunicated if they belong to the syndicates. He has also held a number of masses with Mafia victims, during which he wears Father Peppino's purple stole. In 2015, he traveled to Scampìa outside of Naples, where the Le Vele crack houses are, and met with children of Mafia families under heavy security, telling many in the audience that if they subscribe to a life of crime, the Church has no place for them.[44]

The Camorra is not as sophisticated in structure as the much older Sicilian Cosa Nostra Mafia, which dates back to the late-nineteenth century and is much more famous thanks to its ties to the American Mafia, whose members are Cosa Nostra descendants that emigrated from Sicily, as well as iconic films like *The Godfather*. The Sicilian Mafia operates under a pyramid structure, so when the big boss or "capo" is arrested, he must be replaced. The Camorra is made up of clans and families that share the division of power on a linear scale, which means even multiple arrests won't affect the group's overall power and influence. Families and gangs, known as clans, are loosely connected through alliances based on territories, towns and sectors. The most powerful is the Casalesi clan, which controls the territory around the Land of Fires.

The Camorra's haphazard structure gives way to fierce and often deadly infighting among the clans. But it also allows for individual clans to form alliances – however fragile – with groups like the Nigerian gangs who pose no direct threat to the overall power structure. The Camorra is not the biggest earner of Italy's crime syndicates. That dubious honor goes to the 'Ndrangheta, based in Calabria, which conquered the global heroin and cocaine markets in the nineties when it started importing cocaine directly from Columbia. The European Union's Organized Crime Portfolio estimates that the 'Ndrangheta drug trade accounts for around three percent of Italy's GDP.[45]

Collectively, Italy's recognized organized criminal gangs have an expansive portfolio, between the businesses they have infiltrated and those they run outright. Beyond the lucrative trades in drugs and arms trafficking, the groups also prosper from counterfeiting, construction, racketeering, gambling, money laundering, blackmail, bribery, kidnapping and toxic waste management in addition to extortion, loan sharking and other petty crimes. Essentially, anything illegal.

According to decades of research, Italy's organized crime syndicates rarely deal directly with the sex trafficking and Nigerian sex slavery racket. They will happily take a cut from Nigerian groups that run the racket, but they rarely get into pimping. It's too dirty and in stark contrast to their own views on women and sex. Paying for sex is not something most gangsters think real men should need to do; if a woman won't succumb to their charm, power or money, where is the conquest? Where is the proof of valor? Many crime bosses find the whole business of dealing in the sale of sex rather beneath them, though it would be wrong to say no gangster has ever paid for sex.

There are exceptions, of course, like the well-known case of the enterprising Ukrainian prostitute working along the Domitiana who was shot in both legs in 2014. She was apparently there without a pimp and there was no way to make her pay for her spot on the sidewalk without one, so a Camorra thug shot her, reportedly as a lesson to the Nigerian madams to keep better control of the Domitiana.

There are also instances in Naples where various clans own massage parlors where sex is sold, and at least one "love park" exists in the city, where a Camorra clan member sets up plastic hanging dividers on clothes lines in an abandoned field and Eastern European prostitutes rent compartments for €5 per trick. To keep them honest, the prostitutes are given cellphones and told to send a text message to the clansman whenever they solicit a client so that he can keep an exact tab on how much the women have to pay at the end of every day. The idea of a camera was apparently too invasive, and nothing about the whole setup is apparently illegal enough to prohibit, at least in Naples.

None of that means that they don't get their hands dirty with the exploitation of migrants and refugees. On the contrary, the Camorra and other syndicates make hefty profits from the misery and desperation of those coming to Italy from the sea.

In the summer of 2015, Italian officials found makeshift prisons in a number of southern Italian cities filled with migrants and refugees who had left the authorized camps after their asylum requests had been denied. Most of them were sub-Saharan Africans who were being held until they could be sold into forced labor or until their families at home paid hefty ransoms. One of these squalid prisons near Naples was run by a Camorra clan member and was filled with more than two hundred men and a handful of Nigerian women who hadn't been picked up by madams for sex slavery, either because they were too old or because they had disabilities or other hindrances that would lower their earning potential. They were held in extreme heat with no running water and given only one meal a day. The handful of situations like this that are discovered mean that there are many more that remain hidden.

Italy's ongoing battle with corruption and lawlessness is the base on which all other forms of criminality are built. When one ponders how it can be that such blatant sex trafficking of women can occur in a place like Italy, the only answer can be that the Mafia state that exists allows for it. In essence, the networks of organized crime are a perfect breeding ground for other types of criminality to prosper.

Bullet holes and shrines still mark the spot where six Africans were killed by a Camorra hitman as they tried to escape the Ob Ob Exotic Fashions tailor shop on the Via Domitiana on 18 September 2008.

5

MASSACRES AND ALLIANCES

"Women die out there all the time. They just get rid of
the bodies and no one looks back. There is no one there
to protect the women, and the longer they stay, the more
fear sets into their bones." – Blessing Okoedion, a victim
of sex trafficking turned advocate for victims' rights

CASTEL VOLTURNO – The Ob Ob Exotic Fashions tailor
shop would be out of place almost anywhere in Europe. But it
was especially so along the Domitiana on the outskirts of Castel
Volturno when it opened in the mid-2000s. A thin glass pane
door with peeling white paint opened to a large room with beige
floor tiles and institutional gray walls that took on a lime-green
hue from the buzzing fluorescent lights above. A worn wooden
table in the center of the room was piled high with carefully
folded cloth, some white linen for traditional summer suits,
some colorful African cloth that would soon be transformed
into made-to-measure clothes sewn by the shop's tailor, who
was from Ghana. Two different sized well-worn headless tailor's
mannequins stood in the corner next to a side table with an old
Singer sewing machine.

It was in the center of a strip mall along a rare curve on the
Domitiana, across the street from a large Chinese shop selling
cheap clothing and housewares. The store to the left of the Ob
Ob Exotic Fashions tailor shop still houses a dark, narrow pet
shop that smells of bird droppings and ammonia. A scrawny
Italian woman with visible needle tracks in her thin arms sells

cat litter at the back of the shop, past a wall with noisy song-birds she keeps in tiny rusting cages. The police keep a watch on the pet shop, which is apparently not a pet shop at all, but a cover for something else.

On the other side of what used to be Ob Ob Exotic Fashions is a small beauty parlor with tattered green velvet chairs and tarnished mirrors. It was run by a well-known madam known as Lady Ga Ga, who was said to own around a dozen Nigerian girls whom she would dispatch to parties hosted by wealthy Italians to supplement their work on the sidewalk. She left in 2009, apparently for northern Italy, where she reportedly took a number of her Nigerian women to expand her trade there. Blowjobs are worth €10 on the Domitiana but fetch €5 more in the north.

Now a plump African woman named Betty has the parlour, which is lined with beauty products catering to African women, from hair oils to make-up. The front door to the beauty parlour is made of flimsy Plexiglas, but a back room is secured by a thick security door with double locks. A side door leads to a small, fenced-in yard where a large cappuccino-colored Neapolitan Mastiff guard dog is kept on a worn rope-leash that is not tied to anything in particular.

Betty doesn't take walk-ins in her shop, which is thought to front a connection house that is protected by the security door. A local policeman says Italian men frequently go into the beauty parlor, but rarely come back out with their hair cut. The first time I went to the beauty parlor, identifying myself as a journalist and asking about the history of the Ob Ob Exotic Fashions tailor shop next door, a young girl who couldn't have been more than five years old was sitting in one of the green velvet barber chairs, play-ing with a blonde Barbie doll that had been colored brown with a marker and whose synthetic hair had been braided into tiny corn-rows. When I spoke to her, Betty said she had never heard of the Ob Ob Exotic Fashions tailor shop, despite the fact that the bullet holes are still present on her beauty parlour wall.

When I pressed Betty for more details, a Nigerian man who seemed as wide as he was tall came out from behind the security door and asked me if I needed help. Betty looked down at the floor and the little girl ran out of the side door to play with the dog. I left out of fear and concern that he might think that I was somehow trying to help Betty, who looked afraid. I went back several weeks later. Betty met me at the door and directed me to leave before I could even walk in.

When it first opened, Ob Ob Exotic Fashions was thought to be a cover for the emerging drug trafficking trade run by the Nigerian criminal gangs who had, at that time, just started settling in the area around Castel Volturno. It was shortly after the time when the Camorra started trafficking South American drugs through West Africa to try to get around clampdowns along the traditional routes that had been used to bring the drugs straight to Europe by sea or through other South American ports. It proved much more efficient to go through West Africa because there were fewer controls, which cut down on loss and was much faster. Nigerian and Ghanaian drug traffickers were drawn to this part of Italy based on the sheer volume of drugs they were helping bring in, which seemed to suggest a competitive market.

Many of the Nigerian and Ghanaian men who worked as runners for the Camorra were growing tired of watching the Italian criminals take all the profits. Seeking to cut out the mobsters, the gangs started developing their own competitive racket, charging less than the Camorra because they could bring the drugs in from West Africa themselves.

Local anti-Mafia and anti-drug trafficking authorities across Europe and South America were watching the phenomenon evolve slowly. Then, suddenly, in 2006, the demand for South American drugs in West Africa skyrocketed, implying that the Nigerian racket was taking off.

Rather than intercept the drugs, the cops monitored the shifting movements of the drug trafficking network, trailing many African men they knew ferried the heroin and cocaine for the Camorra and other Italian criminal gangs throughout Europe and beyond. The established alliances seemed to be changing and, with ever more frequency, the drugs went directly to the Nigerian traffickers in and around Castel Volturno, essentially cutting out the Italians who had established the trade in the first place. The police, who understood how the Camorra and the other Mafias worked, were concerned.

There were sporadic arrests of the Nigerian workhorses of the network, but for the most part the intelligence gained from monitoring their activity was far more beneficial than putting two-bit pushers in jail. As it was, much of the activity operated in the open. If more arrests were made, authorities feared they would have pushed the activity further underground, which would have made it harder to monitor.

The emerging drug business in and around Castel Volturno didn't go unnoticed by the Camorra, either. They too were watching the Nigerians develop their own racket. As has long been the case, nothing happens in a criminal syndicate's territory without the express permission of those who control that territory, but the Nigerians hadn't bothered following protocol. Fearful that the business would spread to threaten their long-established heroin trade in nearby Scampìa, local members of the Camorra's Casalesi clan, who ran the territory north of Naples, started threatening the Nigerian drug pushers, demanding they pay a cut of the profits. The Nigerian gangs didn't take them very seriously. Sometimes they paid some of the protection money. Other times they ignored the men who came to collect it.

Whether the Nigerian gang leaders underestimated the power and vengeance of the Camorra or whether they were trying to take over the local trade remains unclear, but at around 9 P.M. on 18 September 2008, on the eve of the religious celebration of the Neapolitan patron saint Gennaro, a car pulled up in front of the Ob Ob Exotic Fashions tailor shop and a hit man pulled out a Kalashnikov and opened fire, killing six African men as they ran from the shop. His associate waited in the getaway car. In all, 120 bullets were spent on the massacre, which lasted only a few minutes.

Within minutes the killers were gone, leaving the dead Africans like a calling card on the sidewalk, which was covered with blood from the spray of bullets. The victims were Samuel Kwaku, twenty-six; Alaj Ababa, thirty-one; Francis Antwi, thirty-one; Eric Affum Yeboah, twenty-five; Alex Geemes, twenty-eight; and Cristopher Adams, twenty-eight. Witnesses who heard the gunfire and saw the river of blood spoke of a scene reminiscent of a war zone.[46]

Twenty minutes before the shooting, the same hit men had taken the life of Antonio Celiento, an Italian man believed to be a police informant who kept tabs on the illegal activity developing in the area. Celiento ran a gaming hall that catered to the growing African community. He was also related to the leader of a rival clan, who was thought to be trying to expand into Casalesi territory. The killers pumped sixty bullets into the Italian's head and stomach before going on to kill the Africans. It was clear that whoever ordered the hit wanted to send a message that they were watching everything going on in and around Castel Volturno.

The main killer was Alfonso Cesarano, a Casalesi gun for hire who was quickly caught at his parents' home, which happened to be next door to Celiento's arcade. The criminal investigation revealed an interesting fact. None of the African men who were murdered were actually affiliated with the Nigerian drug trafficking gangs working to establish business in the area. Instead, they were construction workers from Ghana, Liberia and Togo who mostly did odd jobs for Camorra-controlled companies, according to the memorial obituaries written up for them and posted on the bullet-riddled walls outside the tailor shop. They had met that day at the Ob Ob

Exotic Fashions tailor shop to plan an upcoming religious celebration for their families and children.

The Camorra crime syndicate doesn't make mistakes; they
could have easily murdered Africans who were directly
involved in the drug trade in their coveted territory. The choice
to kill people who were on the sidelines was seen as a combination of a warning and an invitation for collaboration. The
Camorra could clearly see the benefit of working with the
Nigerian gangs, so they were careful not to kill anyone who
might one day be a partner. For one, the Nigerians were
already able to bring the South American drugs through West
Africa to Italy much more cheaply. Second, the Nigerian gangs
had proven themselves to be cunning and deadly, which are
traits the Camorra admires. Collaboration between the two
groups, with the Camorra securely in charge, was a hypothesis
first floated the year before the murders took place by Saviano
in *Gomorrah*. His sources in the area told him that the groups
either had to unite or there would be gang warfare. But even
he was surprised by the violent act, telling me in an interview
at the time that the worst possible scenario would be collaboration between the two groups.

In the days following the mass murder, the African community around Castel Volturno rebelled. Men and women took to
the Domitiana, smashing cars with lead pipes and beating up
local Italians in retaliation. Five Italians affiliated with the
Camorra were eventually arrested in addition to Celiento and
sentenced to more than twenty years in prison. The saga was
memorialized in the award-winning docudrama shot in Castel
Volturno called *La-Bas: Criminal Education* by Guido
Lombardi.

The Italian government sent more than four hundred special
paramilitary troops to the area to patrol the streets, expelling
scores of people who did not have legal working papers and
essentially punishing the African community for the Camorra's
crimes.

Six Italian men ultimately served prison sentences for the murders, but many more Africans were arrested and either jailed or deported during the subsequent riots, which also assured the Camorra that while the authorities may turn a blind eye to their activity, they still won't tolerate an uprising by immigrants.

Eventually the security forces cleared out and the Nigerian criminal gangs went back to trafficking drugs, but not before forging an uneasy alliance with the Camorra that has held despite conventional wisdom that two such powerful and deadly groups cannot work together. The Camorra, having done the killing, was still in charge, and the fact that retaliation for the act was worse for the African community in terms of deportations and arrests meant that the Nigerians had to concede that the Italian criminal group was more powerful.

The deal they forged was simple. In essence, so long as the Nigerians didn't infringe on the Camorra's established clientele and promised to pay a hefty sum of protection money, no one else would get killed. Any missteps would result in another massacre. The money paid for protection meant that the Nigerian gangs had to come up with another form of revenue that didn't eat into their drug trafficking profits. The obvious choice was expanding sex trafficking and debt bondage. They wouldn't be able to exploit Italians or other Europeans, so they exploited their own co-nationals.

The Nigerian women who had come during the early 1980s and 1990s and who were working as prostitutes before the rampant sex trafficking rings were set up teamed up with the Nigerian drug lords to develop the sex slavery scheme that exists today.

With more and more sex workers on the Via Domitiana word soon spread and the area became a magnet for clients looking for cheap sex with black women, which, in a predominantly white mono-cultural society like Italy, was seen as extremely exotic to the Italians, if not taboo. Clients didn't fit any particular character profile. They ranged from young adolescent boys too shy to find girlfriends to old men with wives at home. Businessmen from Naples and Rome came for the sex as well, and soon sex tourists from northern Europe came to stay in the cheap hotels that were popping up along the street.

After the Ob Ob Exotic Fashions tailor shop massacre, the madams, working with human traffickers in Nigeria who were able to tap into the smugglers' network through the Sahara Desert and across the Mediterranean Sea, came up with a payment-plan option of sorts, and soon those who couldn't afford the smuggling charges to get out of Nigeria were told that they could pay it back when they got to Italy, unaware that by the time they arrived the fee would reach €60,000 or more. Most migrants were landing in Southern Italy, where the Nigerian gangs ran the rackets, and so they had the most luck with their own country-women falling for their ruse. Because they were able to make so much money off each girl trafficked for sex, a system was put in place where women in Nigeria who were connected to the madams in Italy actively searched for the most vulnerable women to recruit. Some of the women harbored dreams of leaving Nigeria, where seventy percent of the population lives on less than $1 a day.[47] Others had never even heard of Europe but were convinced they could have a better life after hearing false tales of success of how Nigerian women lived like queens there.

The alliance between the Camorra and the Nigerian gangs continues to hold, but police periodically break up plots by one group against the other. It may seem strange that authorities would spend time keeping peace among the gangs, but, in effect, the status quo keeps the powder keg of criminality from exploding into all-out warfare. Still, the peace is not easy.

The Nigerian gangs are also now considered among the recognized Mafia organizations in Italy. A court in Torino investigating drug and sex trafficking by groups that operate in Sicily and the Land of Fires says that Nigerian gangs operating in Italy are called the "Vatican Family" back home in Nigeria. The gangs originated in Nigeria in the country's university systems, as fraternities, and quickly degenerated to become criminal groups. The gangs have a foothold in many other European countries and the United Kingdom as part of drug-trafficking rings, but their European home is in Italy where they can work with and off the extensive organized crime networks here.

Those who know how to tell the Nigerian gangs apart say the EIYE gang members wear black hats, the AYE wear blue and the Black Axe wear black and red ribbons. An emerging Maphite group, who wear red and green, are generally found near the northern city of Turin. The Black Axe gang was the first to come to Italy, offshoots of a group that originated in rebellious university communities in Nigeria. They focus mostly on trafficking both men and women and achieve this by making sure thousands of women arriving in Italy each year are turned into sex slaves and that the men are shepherded into the drug trade. They deal in heroin and cocaine as well, but their primary source of revenue is the sale of humans.

Until his arrest in March 2016, the leader of the Black Axe gang was a man named Ameyaw Bismark, who went by the name Kelly according to the Neapolitan tribunal document outlining his arrest.[48] He was well-known for brandishing a lead pipe that he used on subordinate gang members and women who weren't working the streets hard enough. He also carried a knife with a serrated blade that left such distinctive wounds on his victims that it acted as a calling card of sorts.

Kelly's second-in-command was Bongo Issaka, and the two were caught on countless tapped cellphone conversations organizing a number of threats for extortion against local businessmen in the area. Just as the Camorra makes its money by charging legitimate Italians protection money, called *pizzo*, the Nigerian gangs have established their own system of profit-taking from the many African businesses that operate for the population in and around Castel Volturno. Their charges include a cut of the sidewalk rent the madams demand from the girls for their tiny spot on the pavement and hefty tariffs for those who operate grocery and clothing stores. Not every African in Castel Volturno is involved in criminality, but there are few who aren't touched by it.

Many Nigerian men also end up in the Black Cats gang, which deals primarily with large orders of illicit drugs and the structural organization of the sex and drug trafficking trades. The organization has its roots in Nigeria, where the main boss is based, and helps facilitate the payment and transport of trafficked women so they don't have to carry money across the desert. If the trafficked women are made to pay expenses upfront, they might be convinced they don't owe their madams money when they get to Italy. Under the current organizational structure, the women rack up the transportation charges, which they promise to pay as part of their JuJu curse.

In Castel Volturno, the top boss of the Black Cats gang is said to be a woman who acts as a liaison between all the various groups and the madams whose profits financially support the overall criminal activity. The Black Cats run a series of businesses including bars and restaurants in the area that police keep under constant surveillance, even as they allow the criminal activity to continue.

Gang members don't use cellphones for criminal business, but communicate primarily face to face or by walkie-talkie radio devices, which makes it hard for the police to monitor them. These gang members favor pistols and switchblades, but have been known to fight with axes. A faction of the gang has migrated to Palermo where they have forged similar ties with the Sicilian Cosa Nostra Mafia. There the mob won't let them use firearms, so the gang members in the emerging Palermo racket can only fight with blades.

The police do intervene from time to time to show their power, but only when they are guaranteed to make the news. In one sting operation by local anti-drug police, a shipment of plaster Madonna figurines was confiscated after a tip-off that the religious icons were filled with crack from Thailand – which they were. The news went viral for obvious reasons.

In 2015, Collins Twumasi went to the police to try to get out of the EIYE gang, detailing for them some of the intricate workings of the organization in exchange for protection and travel documents to stay in Europe. He had tried to leave on his own, but he was beaten and taunted with the tip of an axe, confirmed by his many scars. Twumasi had come to Italy by way of Lampedusa in August 2007 and was transferred to a refugee center in the southern Italian city of Crotone while he waited for his asylum request to be processed. It is illegal to work in Italy during the application-waiting period, but most refugees find odd jobs on the black market, often in the agriculture sector. During his search for a job, he met a man named Kennedy Osazi, who told him there was work in Castel Volturno. Even though his papers hadn't been processed, he left the refugee camp and traveled south by train with Osazi, who he didn't realize was a recruiter for the EIYE.

Once he arrived in Castel Volturno, Osazi told him about the EIYE gang, promising that if he passed the initiation, he could go to work pushing heroin. He'd be given control over a small territory and would have to take out a loan to buy his first supply, but after that, he'd be able to turn a profit, paying only a small fraction to the EIYE.

In time, Osazi told him, he would be able to "buy a girl in Africa and bring her here to earn even more money." Twumasi, out of cash and no longer in line for legitimate documents, says he liked the idea, so he joined Osazi in his drug deliveries to learn the trade. After a few years, Twumasi developed his own customer base. He told police that many of the men purchased women destined for prostitution for as little as €5,000 while they were still in Nigeria and had them delivered to Castel Volturno by smugglers and where they could then be sold to the madams for larger profits, often for around €15,000. The women, he says, had no idea that they were being purchased like slaves. Once the men sold them off, the women would have to pay the madams between €30,000 and €60,000, depending on how much the madams had bought them for from the EIYE gang members.

All Twumasi had to do was come up with the €5,000 to buy his first sex slave. Twumasi soon hooked up with a network of female recruiters working in Nigeria, who charge a finder's fee to locate suitable women for sex work, telling them that they will be hairdressers, if that's the work they are doing in Nigeria, or babysitters if they are unemployed. It is up to the recruiter to determine how much the women have to promise to pay if they ask (many never do), but whatever it is, it is added to the €5,000 fee for getting the girls through Libya. The selling price often includes the added cost of the JuJu curse.

If a woman is particularly beautiful, they often pay less for travel because they will fetch more from the madams, though the men who buy them still pay the same original price. Pictures of the girls, often taken without their knowledge, are posted on private Facebook pages to help finalize the deals, Twumasi told police. The women are then given over to smugglers who are paid by the agents to take them across the Sahara Desert in vans and trucks. Once in Libya, they are sold again to another agent in the network who pays the smugglers to take them across the sea. The conditions are appalling, but the various agents who handle the women have to make sure that they make it to Italy alive, or they risk losing customers in the future.

The first woman Twumasi bought was Blessing Okoedion, a beautiful, statuesque woman who was working in Benin City as a computer technician when she met a recruiter. Blessing happened to be one of the first women I met at Casa Ruth. The recruiting agent, whom Blessing knew as Alice, found her through the local church where Blessing worshipped. She told

Twumasi that because Blessing was educated, she was able to get her a falsified work visa through illicit channels to travel by air, which was not only cheaper than paying the smugglers for land and sea travel, it would ensure her arrival much faster than the six or seven months it often takes for the girls to arrive by the migrant trail.

Alice, the agent in Nigeria sent her first to Spain, as Twumasi tells the story, and then he had her moved to Italy. As Blessing tells the story, she planned to go to Spain after Alice promised her a job with her brother who owned a tech store there. Blessing was excited and set about preparing her documents in Nigeria, getting a certified copy of her diploma and applying for her first passport. Alice took care of the rest, including securing the visa that would allow her to enter Europe legally. But when Alice took her to get her visa in Lagos, the appointment was at the Italian embassy, not the Spanish one, which, at the time, didn't raise a red flag for Blessing. Alice assured her that it was all the same, and that the Italian embassy was just more efficient. Anyway, it was a Schengen visa that would allow her to enter anywhere in Europe.

But when Blessing, accompanied by Alice, arrived at the airport in Benin City, the immigration agent told her the visa was fake. Alice intervened, speaking to the agent (whom she seemed to know) at length. Finally, Blessing was allowed to board the flight. She had a layover in Rabat, Morocco, and then flew to Valencia, Spain, where she passed through passport control without a problem.

She left the arrival terminal thanking God and Alice for the opportunity to start a new life in Europe. She told me she felt complete happiness at that moment. It wouldn't last.

She was expecting to see Alice's brother but, instead, recalls that a woman named Glory picked her up and took her to her house where there were already seven Nigerian women and girls in residence. She was given a room with a fourteen-year-old, a sixteen-year-old and a twenty-two-year-old, who had been there for a month. The morning after Blessing arrived, the oldest of the three left for France.

Blessing started to get concerned. She tried to call Alice in Nigeria, but could get no answer. She asked Glory time and again when she would meet Alice's brother. Finally, Glory told her that Alice's brother had opened a new store in Italy, near Naples, and Blessing would be going there to work. She would be leaving for Naples in the morning. Blessing was concerned about the sudden change, but she agreed to go. After all, she trusted Alice, a woman of God whom she had met at her church. It still had not crossed her mind that she was being trafficked for sex work.

She duly flew to Bergamo the next day and then took a train from Milan to Naples. Glory had arranged all the tickets in advance, and she gave Blessing the number of Alice's brother to call when she arrived in Naples. The man, however, was not Alice's brother. It was Twumasi. He drove her to Castel Volturno where he left her in an apartment with four other girls. She waited three hours and finally a Nigerian couple came to get her. What she didn't know was that while she had been waiting, Twumasi had been selling her to her new madam, who had watched her arrive. Once in the car, a woman, who Blessing now thinks was a sort of fixer for the new girls who had just arrived, and a man, who was a guard to make sure she didn't escape, asked Blessing for her phone to change the SIM card and offered to hold on to her documents for her. She naively handed them over.

Then she asked Blessing: "Do you know what you have to do?"

Blessing said: "Yes, I have to work."

"Yes, you have to hunt men," the woman said.

Blessing laughed. She still hadn't caught on. "How do I do that without a pistol?" she asked, joking.

Then the woman explained that they would soon go shopping for some work clothes and that she had found her a place to work in the mornings, but that they were still looking for a spot for the evenings. Blessing still thought that she would be working in a computer shop.

"How much will I get paid?" she asked.

At this, the man in the car became angry and yelled at her, "We're not paying you. You will be paying us €60,000, and to do that you will have to prostitute yourself."

She wanted to run, but then she remembered that the woman had her phone and documents. Her dreams had been shattered and it was as if the weight of the world had suddenly fallen on her shoulders. The woman then took her to a Chinese shop to buy skimpy clothes. It was March and Blessing didn't want to wear the short skirts and sandals the woman picked out. When she protested, the woman got angry. Soon, Blessing stopped arguing. They left the store and drove back to the apartment where Twumasi had originally left her.

There she met her real madam, whom she was told to call Madam Faith, and who explained to her the work rules. First, she described the various types of police cars, and how she was supposed to run if any potential client opened their car doors, because it was probably an undercover cop. "Clients don't open their doors," Faith told her. She was supposed to charge at least €20 a person, though some might only pay €10 or €15. She must refuse nobody.

Blessing felt deaf, as if everything Madam Faith told her dissipated as soon as the words entered her ears.

She kept repeating that she had not come here to do that sort of work and that Alice in Nigeria had told her that she would be working as a computer technician. Madam Faith only laughed at her. "And you are a graduate," she said, crushing Blessing's confidence.

Madam Faith told her to hide her money in her boot or men who worked for other madams would pretend to be clients and try to steal it from her. She said to be careful if there was more than one person in a car, although not necessarily refuse them because she could charge per person, and that police don't have to pay, especially if they become regular clients. She said not to become friends with the Russian, Ukrainian and Romanian women who worked on the perimeter of the Nigerian women's area, and to let her know if she ever saw one on her section of sidewalk. She told her that if she was scared, she should carry a knife or be prepared to defend herself with a shard of glass. Blessing felt like she was in a nightmare.

She then told Blessing that she should bring clients to the connection house she would be living in, or she could go with them to a hotel, but in any case they had to pay €50 in advance, and that Blessing had to hide the money where they wouldn't find it because, of course, they were always subject to being robbed. Madam Faith gave her a pay-as-you-go cellphone that didn't have enough money on it to make outgoing calls but that she could top up when she started earning.

In addition, Blessing had to pay €150 a month for rental of her sidewalk space, which went directly to the Nigerian gangs with no markup for the madam. Her phone bill, rent and food would be extra. She was told she had to pay €200 a month for her room, €250 a month for utilities, and €50 a week for food. During the winter, she would pay €20 a week for heating. And, most importantly, if she got caught, Blessing should never denounce her or she would come and kill her.

The next day Blessing would start work. Madam Faith stood with Blessing on the street because Blessing didn't speak Italian and helped secure her "first client," with whom Madam Faith arranged to take Blessing to a hotel. He said he was a doctor and spoke English to her. Blessing guessed that he was around fifty years old. He told her he used to work in Nigeria where he learned to like black girls. They went to the hotel and Blessing told him the whole story about Alice, the flight to Spain and arriving in Castel Volturno. They didn't have sex, but the man paid her €50 just the same and left her back on the street. He asked for her phone number and implied that he would try to help her. He never called.

In the days that followed, Blessing had no choice but to sell her body under threat of rape and other violence. She did it reluctantly, hoping to find men like her first client who would listen to her story instead of using her body. Instead, she soon realized she was just merchandise, a machine for sex, a piece of meat.

When she finally earned money, her madam took it directly from her purse the minute she walked into the connection house so she couldn't stash any for herself. Blessing knew she needed money to leave, so she tried to hide some the next day. After her second day on the street, she decided to find a police station. She searched and searched, but she dared not ask any of the other girls because it was hard to know which women were madams keeping an eye on their girls.

Finally, she met a Nigerian man who, like her, was educated in Nigeria but had fallen into drug trafficking with the Nigerian gangs. She asked him to take her to the police station, but he was afraid of being arrested or, worse, that a fellow gang member would see him. Instead, he told her where it was. Not speaking a word of Italian, when she arrived the police officer told her to come back the next morning at 9 A.M., when someone could speak to her in English. She returned to the street.

The next morning, she got to the station at 9 A.M. and there was an English-speaking officer there. She signed a complaint against Alice, Madam Faith and her husband and the police took her to Casa Ruth. She was off the street just four days after she arrived.

Many women have successfully left the street, but Blessing has become a sort of spokesperson for the work that Sister Rita and the other nuns and volunteers do, and, in 2017, she published an autobiography with Italian journalist Anna Pozzi, who has dedicated her career to covering the Catholic Church's role in helping sex trafficked women. Their book, called *The Courage of Freedom*, follows Blessing's story from Nigeria, and underscores the frustrations she feels that she can't do more.

Because Blessing was not tied to the sex trade or to her madam by the JuJu curse, and because she did not integrate with the rest of the girls on the streets who often affirm each other's fears of leaving, she is somewhat of an anomaly among sex-trafficked women. Her story is one of the few with a relatively happy ending in this horrific racket, but she still struggles with what she has been through. Twumasi, despite his testimony that has been corroborated by Blessing, is still in jail.

Blessing now works as a cultural mediator with Nigerian migrants who arrive in Italy by boat, but it is far too dangerous for her to return to the Domitiana to try to convince young women that they can leave. While neither her madam nor Alice were ever arrested for what they put her through, the fact that she has denounced them has earned a price on her head, and she knows it. "Women die out there all the time," she tells me. "They just get rid of the bodies and no one looks back. There is no one there to protect the women, and the longer they stay, the more fear sets into their bones."

Blessing is an integral part of Casa Ruth and the sisters often call her when traumatized young women arrive. But despite all the obvious good she does, she is often frustrated that all her efforts are just a drop in the ocean. Sister Rita says that in her more than twenty years working with women from the Domitiana, she has never met anyone like Blessing. "She is a unique gem," she says. "She is very special and she will be the one to make a difference in this horrible trade if she is given the right opportunity."

Sitting in Sister Rita's study one winter afternoon, Blessing grew angry that no one warns young women in Nigeria about what is happening. She says the Nigerian embassy in Rome, too, knows what is going on but are complicit in the racket. In fact, my own attempts to interview someone at the Nigerian embassy about the eleven thousand women who arrived in Italy in 2016 were met with ambivalence. That question, they said, had to be answered in Nigeria at the Italian consulate. But when I reached the Italian consulate, they referred me to the Nigerian interior ministry. When I reached them, they referred me again to the Italian consulate, which sent me back to the Nigerian embassy in Rome.

Blessing and the journalist Pozzi traveled back to Nigeria with the Catholic Church's anti-trafficking group Slaves No More, run by Sister Eugenia Bonetti in Rome. They met Blessing's family in the village and set up engagements to speak about trafficking at churches in Benin City. But Blessing couldn't speak about trafficking in her own village. She had told her younger sisters about what had happened so that the same thing wouldn't happen to them, but she has not told her parents, who she says would surely feel as if it was their fault. She kept with her original story when she saw them, that her job as a computer technician that she left for was going well.

When she returned to her muddy village, she saw more clearly the circumstances that made her so vulnerable in the first place. None of her old peers truly understood the reality of life in Europe; they all had grandiose ideas of what it was really like. She couldn't blame them. Sitting in her parent's hut, she remembered thinking the same thing.

But what most infuriates Blessing and others who escape sexual slavery is how hard it is to convince women in Nigeria that they are all vulnerable. Even Blessing's own sister, who, despite knowing all she had been through, called her one day after she returned to Italy to tell her what she thought was great news. She had met a woman whose brother wanted to hire her as a babysitter in London. Blessing's younger sister even saw pictures of the family for whom she would be working. Blessing was incredulous. "There is no job as a babysitter," she screamed over the phone to her sister. "There is only one kind of work in Europe for Nigerian women."

The Land of Fires, and more specifically the Domitiana, is the epicenter for the Nigerian gangs and the forced sex-slave market, but it is not the only area where these rackets are in place. In many ways, Sicily is an emerging market for the Nigerian gangs who have only recently made inroads with the Sicilian Cosa Nostra to collaborate with large-scale drug and sex-trafficking rings there. Their induction into the Sicilian organized-crime world was not as bloody as that of their partners in Castel Volturno, undoubtedly because of the lessons learned by the Nigerians at the hands of the Camorra. When the Nigerian gangs first set up in Sicily, they went straight to the Mafia to ask for permission and collaboration. The Sicilian Mafia granted it under several conditions: they stay away from established Cosa Nostra business, pay the protection money and don't use guns. As a result, disputes among gang members in Sicily can only be resolved with knives and axes.

Even before the Nigerian gangs set up an organized sex-trafficking ring in Sicily, random Nigerian madams kept girls on the streets across the island just as they do in almost every urban area in Italy. They are usually under the control of one or two madams who keep a handful of girls in cities like Catania, Agrigento, Syracuse and Palermo, which has the highest concentration on the island. Around five hundred Nigerian women are thought to be working on the streets and in illegal brothels there. Many can be found on the streets that traverse the Parco della Favorita, an overgrown park littered with garbage, condoms and syringes that offers secluded areas for blowjobs and discreet alcoves for sex in cars. Police turn a blind eye there, only patrolling the streets to answer specific calls.

The upturn in the number of Nigerian women being trafficked for sex in Palermo started in 2012, around the same time but not at the same level as Castel Volturno. The Sicilian Cosa Nostra had not allowed the presence of foreign criminal gangs – they just didn't fit into the hierarchy – so the Nigerians were not able to set up the same trafficking racket as they did in Camorra territory.

That year, a number of young Nigerian women were killed. One, named Favour Nike Adekunle, who had arrived by way of Lampedusa months earlier, was found dead in Parco della Favorita. She had been strangled and badly burned. Her corpse had started to decompose in the woods when she was eventually found; it had been a long time before anyone had noticed she was missing, despite the fact that she had told friends that she had a Sicilian boyfriend who, if she was telling the truth, would have surely raised the alarm. Favour's body was left in a refrigerator at the Palermo city morgue for two years while an investigation into her death stalled. It was never a priority. By the time they released her body to members of the Nigerian community for burial, there were only a few bones left. Someone had stolen most of her corpse. Investigators later concluded that her assailant was likely a Sicilian Mafioso who killed her when her madam wouldn't pay him a cut of her earnings.

A few days after Favour's body was found, Loveth Edward, a fifteen-year-old Nigerian girl, was found murdered in Palermo with a note on her body that said she had died for "the sins of her mother." She had apparently been a sex slave who was hiding money from her madam.

Since that time, the Palermo sex-trafficking rings have become more organized because the Cosa Nostra, like the Camorra, has allowed for collaboration with the Nigerians in the drug trade. And, like the Camorra, the Cosa Nostra requires protection money that can be made easily on the backs of the girls. Since most of the women rescued from the smugglers' boats start in Sicily, it's only natural that they would eventually be exploited there, too. The same Nigerian gangs that operate in Castel Volturno operate in Sicily, which makes them the only common denominator among the various Italian Mafias, which do not openly collaborate.

Many of the girls have been moved from the Parco della Favorita to the dark streets of Palermo's Ballarò market area, where they are forced to take men to small first-floor apartments that double as crack houses. The whole area is a vibrant vegetable and fish market by day but turns dangerous rather quickly by nighttime. During a visit with an undercover police officer in 2015, I saw a Nigerian woman dressed in a sequin tank top and matching thong with a leash around her neck tied to a streetlamp post. She was on her knees giving blowjobs to maybe a dozen or more men who had lined up around the corner. None appeared to be wearing a condom. The woman, who kept her eyes closed tight, gagged loudly as the men forced their penises into her mouth. She spat the ejaculate on the ground in front of her as the next client unzipped his pants. Another woman, presumably her madam, collected money from those in the line. The police officer said there was nothing necessarily illegal about what was going on, although sex in public is theoretically a crime. "They shouldn't really be outside," he said. "But who hasn't had a blowjob in the open before?"

In November 2016, sixteen members of the same Black Axe gang that operates in Castel Volturno, along with a Nigerian madam, were arrested in Palermo on charges of drug and sex trafficking, and for particularly gruesome sexual violence against men and women. A male victim, a refugee who had gained political asylum but who would not join the Black Axe gang, was "anally raped for a whole night with an iron pipe," according to the complaint read in a court hearing I attended in Palermo. He had to have multiple surgeries to repair his rectum. The complaint also listed several incidents of gang rape and sexual torture involving objects against a number of underage Nigerian girls who refused to prostitute themselves. One victim was raped so violently she ended up in a coma; another nearly bled to death. A third is now in psychiatric care.

A few months before the trial of the lead-pipe assailant,

Yusapha Susso, a Ghanaian asylum seeker who was a customer at the Ballarò drug market, was shot in the back of the head. The fact that he was killed with a gun and not a knife told investigators that it was the work of the Sicilian Mafia, not the Nigerians. The man arrested was a local Sicilian Mafia thug, thought to have carried out the act in an attempt to instill a little bit of order in the Ballarò district and to show that the Italians were still in charge.

In fact, Guido Longo, the police commissioner in Palermo, told me on the sidelines of a court hearing in early January 2017 that the Cosa Nostra risk losing power to the Nigerians, though they would never admit it. "As more migrants arrive and join the Nigerian gangs, the Cosa Nostra will have a hard time staying in control," he said. "When that happens, we could see gangland warfare in Palermo like we've never seen before."

The police are prepared for just that, but it will be the Nigerians who face the biggest consequences, just as they did in Castel Volturno when the riots ensued after the Ob Ob Exotic Fashions tailor shop massacre. The Cosa Nostra has reigned over Sicily for far too long to give up its turf so easily. For years, it was able to keep migrants and any foreign criminal groups at bay, but the sheer number of arrivals and the power of the Nigerian gangs are just too great now, which could forever change the dynamic of organized crime in Italy. In many ways, the recent influx already has.

A worrying trend in the uneasy partnership between the emerging Nigerian gangs and the established organized-crime syndicates is the disappearance of thousands of unaccompanied African minors who arrive in Italy each year. Europol estimates that more than ten thousand unaccompanied minors who have arrived by sea to Italy since 2015 have disappeared without a trace. Many of them will have met family members, but many more are feared to have been sucked into criminal networks. Young women invariably end up in forced sex work;

young men as petty criminals for the country's various mobs, including the Nigerian gangs.

No matter which crime syndicate's territory they are shackled to, the Nigerian sex slaves and the profits they generate provide important revenue, comprising more than eighty percent of the country's paid sex market.[49] The Nigerian sex-trafficking racket turns over an estimated profit of around €2 billion a year in Italy (with the entire industry turning over around $99 billion globally).[50] There is no way to know for sure just how many Nigerians are forced to sell sex in Italy at the hands of the criminal gangs because they are living in the shadows, but some estimate that there could easily be thirty or forty thousand women in Italy alone. How many more are spread across Europe is unimaginable.

Eastern Europeans and women from the former Soviet Bloc have also become increasingly common in the sex industry in Italy and, in recent months, the Nigerian madams have allowed them, along with cross-dressing and transgender prostitutes, to rent space on the Via Domitiana and in other territories they control. However, as they bring in a mere fraction of the business the Nigerian sex workers do, they can only use the tightly controlled sidewalk space during irregular hours, like mornings and early afternoons.

It's hard to understand just why Nigerian women are so vulnerable to the sex trafficking trade. Carlotta Santarossa, a counter-trafficking project manager for the International Organization on Migration, says their group provides legal information and counseling for women when they arrive by sea. They give out brochures that point out tell-tale signs of sex trafficking and they offer legal counseling for women who want to denounce their traffickers. The problem is that when they first arrive, most women are so traumatized as a result of their torturous time in Libya, their rough sea voyage and the fact that they might have very nearly drowned, that they don't understand the circumstances in which they now find themselves. "They might know what trafficking is, but they often don't think it is happening to them," she told me. "The system is well-known by all and well structured. It preys on poor families and uneducated women, and it is extremely hard to break."

Santarossa says many of the women are so embarrassed that they've been duped into trafficking, they can't bring themselves to tell their families what is happening, which further isolates them. "They feel it is their duty to send back money; [it's] their opportunity to help their families," she says. "Then when they realize what has happened, they don't know how to come to terms [with the situation]."

One of the ruined apartment blocks in the Coppola Village where arms are stashed and drugs are sold. Scores of squatters, including African migrants and sex-trafficked women, live in these condemned buildings.

6

KALASHNIKOVS AND BODIES UNDER THE MATTRESSES

"I was afraid to perform certain sex acts for fear the weapons would explode under the bed." – "Holly," a trafficked woman

DRUGS

VOLTURNO DESTRA – The Boomerang Hotel was once a boxy three-star property along the Domitiana just outside the Coppola Village. Hotel guests passed through tall iron gates to a parking lot that opened up to a wide, bleached cement sidewalk leading up to the hotel. The set-up was meant to give the air of an exclusive hideaway tucked among large umbrella pines and manicured hedges. The hotel's large foyer opened up to an oval swimming pool with a smaller circular hot tub on one end that made it look somewhat like a snowman.

A trail carved out of the pine forest still winds its way from the pool area to what was once a private beach, where guests could lounge in matching sun chairs. Now the trail is strewn with syringes and the former sunning area is awash with garbage and raw sewage that is pumped out to sea from the abandoned Coppola apartment blocks down the road and floats back in with the tide. Inside the hotel foyer, square columns jut from terracotta tile floors that were inlaid with tacky designs

depicting Greek and Roman gods. Recreations of famous frescoes are cracked and peeling on the arched ceilings overhead.

Though it's hard to believe now, the Boomerang Hotel was
once a popular weekend getaway, where middle-class Romans
and Neapolitans could bring their mistresses. It was closed for
good in the mid-2000s, confiscated as part of a crackdown on
the Camorra's illegal land grab.

Now, the abandoned structure is a popular crack house. At
least once a year, police conduct raids and routinely find the
stiff bodies of dead drug addicts in rooms that used to be the
upstairs suites. Sometimes the squatters call the cops and then
disappear while they come to collect the corpses. Other times,
when the rotting smell becomes overwhelming, they drag the
bodies out into the forest. Once, a man with the syringe still
stuck in his vein under a tourniquet was carried out to sea with
the tide. He washed back up a few miles down the beach, and
though the authorities assumed he came from the Boomerang,
he could equally have died at any of the similar crack houses
along the beachfront.

In 2014, a raid of the hotel netted twenty-one Nigerian men
who were thought to be local drug bosses working out of the
Boomerang. The cops condemned the old hotel once again,
boarding up the open doors and windows with plywood and
cement blocks. Within a week, however, the new drug bosses
had knocked through the boards with a sledgehammer and it
was back open for business.

Piles of plastic syringes and empty Coke bottles float on the
dark green algae in the abandoned swimming pool, now fed by
winter rains. Overgrown yucca trees bend and twist across the
hotel's main entrance. Dazed men walk around the structure
like zombies, maintaining a mind-bending high with regular
trips to the lower levels, where the drugs are sold in one-hit
doses.[51]

Outside, the used plastic syringes crunch like frozen snow
under foot. A thick carpet of used clothing and food wrappers

covers the cement floors. Stacks of bricks have been assembled to form makeshift toilets in the former upstairs bathrooms in an abandoned wing of the hotel. Every now and then someone scoops up the odorous feces with a stained shovel that leans against the wall and throws it out of the window into the garden below.

Drying laundry, some of it so old it is covered in mold, hangs on rudimentary clotheslines strung along the fences outside and across some of the now glassless windows upstairs. The once-manicured gardens have been invaded by plastic bottles, empty tinfoil rolls and human and dog excrement. Pieces of torn up foam mattress are scattered everywhere like confetti. The stench of urine, unwashed bodies and rotting food is almost overwhelming, but none of the regular residents seem to notice. Stray dogs and cats with matted fur wander in and out of the building, nibbling on crumbs left for them by the addicts.

Most days, an older Nigerian woman named Sally brings in rice dishes and other meals she sells for a few euro a plate. Some of the Domitiana girls have a permanent presence in the former concierge rooms where mattresses are spread out on the floors to cater to the addicts who want more than just drugs. Most of these women are addicts, too, essentially spending what's left after they've paid their madams with the pushers who operate on the lower floors. It is an uneasy place to visit, even with an undercover police officer, made more so by the fact that no one is sober or aware enough really to notice us.

As many as fifty people sleep at the Boomerang most nights, many of whom also work as drug mules for the Nigerian gangs by day. The Boomerang is in the part of Castel Volturno known as the "Volturno Destra" on the right side of a river that divides the town in half and spills into the sea. It is the epicenter of the degradation and Nigerian-led lawlessness that Italians try to avoid.[52] Police keep an eye on what's going on, but don't do much to stop it because it's more useful to them to use the

Nigerian criminals to keep an eye on the Camorra's drug-trafficking activities.

The Camorra drug trade easily prospers in this part of the Land of Fires with the help of the Nigerian gangs, running a monthly profit of well over $10 million, according to the United Nations Office of Drugs and Crime (UNODC). Their business model is based on catering to addicts, selling heroin and a very pure crack cocaine that is known on the street as "zero zero zero" (000), the European bakers' term for the finest grade of flour available on the market.

The UNODC monitors both small and large-scale shipments of South American drugs into Europe, which they say are now mainly transported by way of West Africa, where the Nigerians based in and around Castel Volturno originated. Most of the trafficking is done by private aircraft from Columbia and Venezuela straight to Nigeria, Ghana and other West African nations.[53] From there the drugs are smuggled into Italy and Spain by land, air or sea. Authorities say that the Camorra and Italy's other crime gangs increasingly rely on their Nigerian collaborators to facilitate the smuggling. Once on the European continent, the drugs are trafficked by Italians and some Eastern Europeans working for the Camorra to the United Kingdom, France and Germany – which, along with Italy and Spain, account for seventy-five percent of the European market.

Larger quantities of the drugs are creatively hidden in containers on cargo ships that dock at ports in southern Italy, Spain and Gibraltar.[54] Authorities don't rule out the movement of smaller quantities of drugs across the Sahara, which has been a merchant route for illicit goods and migrating people since record-keeping began. Trafficked women have also admitted to carrying moderate stashes of cocaine across the desert. Those who do it say they were told it would pay for their transit, although the credit never seems to be applied to their final debts.

Still, the UNODC says no large-scale seizure of drugs or other contraband has ever occurred in the Sahara Desert, although that is likely due to a lack of vigilance rather than the absence of smuggling. Patrolling the desert routes for drugs would also help stop the trafficking of women to Europe, though such initiatives are never even mentioned when authorities meet to discuss what can be done to combat the problem.

The growing presence of ISIS militants in Libya makes the desert transit risky for drug traffickers as well, since the group has been known to overlook their own prohibition of drug use and steal the drugs to sell in the areas they control to fund their fight against the West, though they generally leave the trafficked Nigerian women alone.[55] The United States Drug Enforcement Agency (DEA), which follows several different drug trafficking routes, says that ISIS militants often "tax" the shipments that cross through their territory, claiming that, in 2016, seven percent of ISIS revenue in Libya came directly from the production, taxation or trafficking of drugs. Other militia groups operating in Libya hold the drug shipments hostage, demanding handsome ransoms. Everyone, it seems, has found an opportunity to make money on the trade in one way or another.

Since Libya has turned into a failed state under the control of a handful of militia groups, drugs are also believed increasingly to be flown straight into Libyan airports on small aircraft from West African nations. Sometimes the drugs are then moved by complicit fishermen and luxury yacht operators who can easily navigate between North African and Italian and Spanish ports without raising suspicion. These types of drug smugglers are often paid in cocaine, which deters theft and essentially makes them business partners. It also means they will take the fall alone if they get caught.

Not all drug shipments go through West Africa and Libya to get to Europe, however. In early 2017, Italian authorities, who had been tracking a freighter suspected of carrying drugs directly to Italy from Brazil, confiscated $84 million worth of pure cocaine bundled into seventeen waterproof bags. The crew had tossed the cargo into the sea south of Naples, near the notorious port of Gioia Tauro in Calabria. The waterproof parcels were attached to buoys and had GPS trackers. Officials implicated the 'Ndrangheta Mafia based in Calabria, which came into the drug market late, but has quickly become the worldwide leader in cocaine trafficking, followed by the Camorra, according to the Italian police's annual report on the global drug trade.

Part of the 'Ndrangheta's success comes from a business model that relies on emigrating mobsters into Latin America. By sending the Mafiosi there to help set up the networks and guide the trafficking, they have been able to reach an astonishing level of financial success, bringing in around $66 billion in drug revenue a year and controlling more than eighty percent of Europe's drug trade, according to UNODC – not bad for a group of gangsters who started as small-time thugs kidnapping businessmen from rich families for ransom money. The 'Ndrangheta is not yet known to have made an alliance with Nigerian gangs, and the presence of trafficked women is rare in the deep southern regions of Calabria. On one hand, there is a distinct lack of clientele there, and on the other, 'Ndrangheta men are very particular about women, and are staunchly against paying for sex out of basic masculine pride.

Once the drugs arrive in Italy, the distribution networks are well-oiled machines. Nowhere is that more apparent than in and around Naples. For years, the Camorra ran their operations out of a pyramid-shaped housing complex called Le Vele ("The Sails") in the rundown suburb of Scampìa, north of Naples.

I visited Le Vele in 2008 for a story for *Newsweek* magazine just after Matteo Garrone's film *Gomorrah*, based on Saviano's book, came out.[56] I was at once struck by the open criminality I witnessed there; so arrogant no one even tried to hide it from the cameras. There was no fear of getting caught, no sense that what was going on was particularly wrong. Many of the corridors and walkways through the complex had heavy gates that could swing and lock automatically in seconds, installed by the Camorra to keep out the cops.

I went with a Neapolitan photographer recommended to me by Saviano, who said he could get me in and out. I paid €87 in protection money to Lorenzo Lipurali, a chubby man in a Napoli soccer team sweatshirt who acted as our tour guide.

While we were there, a television crew from France was held up at knifepoint in another part of the complex. They apparently refused to pay any protection money, so the Camorra thugs collected it their own way.

The whole complex, condemned for destruction, was impeccably clean despite the bullet-ridden windows and mice that scurried freely through the corridors. Those who live there are squatters who have rigged up electrical systems, heating and sewage along the lines of what is set up in the Coppola ruins in Castel Volturno, in a practice that is common in the poorest parts of southern Italy. Mr. Lipurali's apartment smelled like ammonia and pine cleaner, and his impeccably groomed fourteen-year-old daughter Anna served us coffee out of tiny plastic cups that were later discarded out of the windows. In a surreal moment, Mr. Lipurali pulled out a bootlegged copy of Garrone's film and slipped it into a DVD player attached to a massive flatscreen television in his living room. Suddenly, the same scene I could see from outside his window was playing on the TV. He fast-forwarded to the part where he played himself as a resident helping neighbors move a giant sofa down several floors with a rope.

Later that day, I bought my own bootlegged copy of *Gomorrah* from an African vendor on the Via Roma in Naples for three euro, a sort of souvenir from a strange assignment I was quite relieved to have survived unscathed.

Saviano, by then, was under police escort with a Camorra death sentence hanging over his head, but the truth of the matter was that everyone I met around that area sort of liked the infamy that his account of their miserable lives gave them. Mr. Lipurali's fifteen seconds of fame were a defining moment for him, a lifetime achievement of sorts, despite the irony of playing himself as a lowlife thug.

Mr. Lipurali took us down to the basement where the heroin shots were sold to those waiting in expensive SUVs, scooters and beat-up Fiats double-parked outside. There was a fold-up table where a clearly stoned woman sold Coca Cola, chocolate bars and syringes for one euro each. Kids who live in the complex came down to buy the soda and chocolate, often waiting in line behind the staggering drug addicts there for the heroin.

In 2012, anti-drug police conducted a series of raids of the basements of Le Vele, arresting scores of pushers and their clients and vowing to level the complex, although at the time of writing in 2017 it is still standing. The arrests only served to push the open-market drug trade to the nearby village of Afragola under a similar setup, in the process giving more business to the Nigerians in Castel Volturno.

The Nigerians sell cocaine and heroin in Castel Volturno for slightly cheaper prices than the Camorra, even though they give a cut of the profits in the form of protection money or *pizzo* to the Camorra. Aside from the fact that no one would expect to pay the Nigerians the same price they pay Italians, which is a theory held in the sex trade as well, a reason for this discrepancy in price is the direct connections to the sources in South America they have through contacts in West Africa. Another reason is that they are said to cut the drug with "fillers," which decreases the quality and the production costs. Nigerian cocaine does not share the Camorra's "000" ranking.

The customers who prefer the Nigerian drug market often combine the drugs with sex, taking advantage of the availability of sex slaves along the Domitiana. It is common for connection houses to work with drug dealers and vice versa to make it easy for customers to do one-stop shopping. The Nigerians also supply other pushers, African and otherwise, who buy large and medium quantities to distribute across Italy and Europe.

Italy's organized crime groups are fierce competitors with one another, but they all take advantage of the same weak links in Italy's corrupt systems. They all exploit the incoming migrants by siphoning funds off the shelters and they all work around Italy's weak tax structure that makes it easy to launder money and avoid taxes. The reason these powerful syndicates are allowed to exist is because the country's leaders don't have the resolve to stop them either out of fear or affiliation.

The whole drug-selling set-up is a perfect example of how easy it is to operate outside the law in southern Italy. It is well documented by a wide range of authorities, which can't effectively stop it because its roots are buried too deeply in the Neapolitan and Italian DNA. The drug trade, just like the sex trafficking racket, is too vast to root out easily. Most of the drugs are stored in small parcels in houses owned by local people who aren't even part of the Camorra but who rent out their basements and storage rooms for extra cash. It's not easy to say no to the Camorra, so few do. The sense of obligation and omertà is too strong to fracture. More than that, fear of death tends to keep people quiet and cooperative.

Little goes on in Castel Volturno without the police knowing. Sex trafficking is of course against the law, but since prostitution is legal, police more often than not turn a blind eye to the sordid details about how the women get there, even though they know blatant exploitation is ruining scores of lives. Nazzaro, the journalist and Five-Star spokesman who grew up in the area, points out that it takes at least three people to save a Nigerian from her pimp: a translator, a lawyer and an immigration specialist who can determine if the woman should be deported due to false documents or taken to a shelter like Casa

Ruth. Police, instead, tend to deal with more acute problems, like murders, which can happen at a rate of around ten a month at the hands of the Camorra.

ARMS

A bigger priority for authorities than the illicit drugs and sex trades is the fast-growing illegal arms trade that police say is tied to terrorist groups sympathetic to ISIS.[57] Police have found scores of caches of weapons and munitions buried in the Camorra hinterland, ready for pick-up by mercenaries they believe are headed north to Germany, France, Belgium and the UK to carry out attacks. It is no great coincidence that Italy's anti-terrorism and anti-Mafia investigators are one and the same. It would be redundant to separate the two investigative arms.

Italians like to use the word *malaffare*, which translates to "malfeasance," or "wrongdoing," in English, and they often use it to describe illegal activity linked to the accepted cultural norms, such as corruption in the public and private sector as well as all that is tied to organized crime in southern Italy. Enzo Di Ciaccio is a veteran Italian journalist who has spent his long career chronicling the *malaffare* of the criminal world in the Land of Fires. He is lucky to be alive and he knows it. He is effectively embedded with the various clans of the Camorra, and as such is able to operate much like a war correspondent who becomes trusted as he follows the same battalions in conflict. They don't always like what he writes, but he's still alive, which is a show of respect of sorts.

He calls Castel Volturno the "ideal refuge for the desperate of the southern hemisphere," describing it as a perfect training ground for "terrorists and aspiring jihadists, where black prevails over white, where one lives without rules, and where the Italian state has abdicated any kind of presence." He is quick to point out that nowhere else in Italy is there a community in which the majority of its population consists of documented or undocumented Africans. That, he says, combined with such a strong criminal presence like the Camorra, makes it an anomaly that authorities find almost impossible to control, in part because they just don't know how. They have no power over either group.

He and others have pointed to faulty legislation that makes arms smuggling relatively easy and risk-free. Italy is a major producer of weapons – the seventh largest exporter in the world in 2016 – which means all kinds of weapons are readily available, though they can't easily be sold on the black market because those produced legally are well documented. To facilitate the importation of certain components needed to build these arms for export without tedious customs forms and permission requests, Italian customs don't prohibit bringing in the individual pieces of weapons of war, so long as they come into the country deconstructed. On his blog, *Lettura 43*, Ciaccio mocks the existing laws. "Just pack up pieces of pistols, rifles, machine guns and Kalashnikovs because they are considered harmless metallic carpentry and escape any serious controls."

He's right. There is nothing that prohibits anyone with a license to import goods for metallic carpentry used in factories and other legitimate businesses from legally importing the components that are necessary to build weapons. The Camorra has scores of shell companies with valid licenses in almost every sector, including those that allow for the importation of metallic carpentry. All they have to do is put the pieces together and they have undocumented weapons to sell to terrorists and others who can't buy weapons legitimately.

Police discovered a weapons cache they believe was earmarked for foreign fighters during an armed robbery arrest of a Nigerian man who was hiding out at a connection house in Castel Volturno in early 2016. It included live grenades and rocket launchers that had been hidden under the bed in the same house where women were forced to return with their tricks. "I was afraid to perform certain sex acts for fear the weapons would explode under the bed," one of the women who lived in the house told police.

Another woman reported that the guns were left there by Italian men who owned the house, presumably Camorra thugs. The woman, whom I will call Holly to protect her identity, said they were to be picked up by Nigerian gang members who police believe would take them north into Europe. Often police have to rely on the testimony of victims of sex trafficking, who are invariably afraid to tell the whole truth out of fear of retaliation. The secretive nature of most of what happens in the area makes it hard to come by reliable information. *Pentiti*, the Italian word for a turncoat or defector who is still alive after leaving a life of crime, are few and far between.

One witness who has been particularly reliable is a former child soldier from Liberia who was working for a Nigerian gang before he started trading police protection for his first-hand testimony, making him a crucial attester to how the emerging weapons trade is tied to the migrant crisis. According to his testimony in a March 2017 arrest warrant for a group of twenty-three Nigerian men, which led to one of the biggest arms cache discoveries near Castel Volturno to date, the Nigerian gangs are well equipped in reassembling weaponry, which allows them to help the Camorra turn bit parts into an extremely lucrative business.

The former child soldier, who is often referred to as "Jo" in investigative reports, warned Italian police about incoming terrorists more than a decade ago when he first started working with the police as an informant. "There are people who have been part of Boko Haram and who now live here even though it is not easy to locate them. They have the ability to provide support to terrorists in attacks and also take advantage of others," he told anti-Mafia investigators, according to official documents. "Everyone knows how to move the weapons here and everyone knows how to assemble them. Often they bury them in the grounds of the Castel Volturno area to be picked up later."

In 2015, Neapolitan police arrested a Nigerian man as he approached a buried arms cache they had under surveillance. Police nabbed him before he retrieved any weapons out of an abundance of caution, fearful that the cache might explode or that they might get caught up in a gun battle with others who might be waiting for him if they hesitated too long. Had they let him pick up the arms instead, he might have led them to the foreign fighters waiting for the arms delivery, but as it played out, they just didn't want to risk a firefight or ambush.

They were sure the arms were intended for foreign trade, however. Because Camorra hits tend to be personal and directed at only one person, they can generally be carried out with pistols, often fitted with silencers. An exception is when they intend to carry out massacres meant to draw attention, like the Ob Ob Exotic Fashions tailor shop killings when they used a Kalashnikov. Terrorists, as was demonstrated in both the Paris and Brussels attacks of 2015 and 2016 respectively, tend toward semi-automatic weapons like Kalashnikov rifles that can kill a large number of people at once. The weapons cache outside of Naples included more than a dozen Russian-made Kalashnikovs that are thought to have come into Italy from the Balkans during the late nineties.

In February 2017, an Italian couple in their sixties who had been radicalized was arrested south of Naples for trafficking arms and helicopters to terrorists in Iran and Libya.[58] Mario di Leva, sixty-nine, and his wife Anna Maria Fontana, sixty-three, had converted to Islam back in the 1980s. Authorities say Di Leva, who adopted the name Jaafar, had turned to radical Islam a decade later. His wife followed suit, earning her the nicknames "Veiled Lady" and "Dark Lady." Di Leva was an outspoken Freemason before converting to Islam; his wife a councilwoman who had at one time worked to expose businesses with ties to the Camorra, although the cops suspected even at the time that she was a double agent. Their alleged accomplices were Andrea Pardi, who owned a local Italian helicopter dealership, and their son Luca di Leva, along with Ali Mohamud Shaswish, a Libyan middleman whose whereabouts are as yet unknown.

The arms trafficking couple allegedly had also helped to create an elaborate scheme to import weapon parts to the Camorra, according to ongoing investigation. They specialized in components for Kalashnikovs, pistols and automatic weapon magazines from Nigeria, Somalia, Sudan, Libya and Iran, which the Camorra could then have their Nigerian counterparts assemble so they could sell to foreign fighters throughout Europe. It was a way of getting the weapons into Italy easily through the ports without technically breaking any customs laws should the authorities check.

The couple first appeared on the anti-terrorism radar after Di Leva posted incriminating comments on his Facebook page, essentially mourning the loss of Colonel Gaddafi, whom they described as a "dear friend," after he was killed in Libya. To be fair, it wasn't altogether odd for an Italian to lament Gaddafi's passing. After all, the two countries had enjoyed mutually beneficial trade agreements thanks to Berlusconi. There was something a little too intimate about Di Leva's posts, however, that caused police to suspect that something was amiss. Nonetheless, they had no reason to suspect the couple of any crimes until 2015, when four Italian oil workers were kidnapped by ISIS militants in Libya, many of whom would be eventual recipients of the couple's illicit arms and helicopters.

Investigators immediately suspected that the kidnappings were an inside job, organized by criminals in Italy, either as a way to extort money for ransom from the Italian government or to gain control of lucrative oil fields in Libya that had been developed by both private and public Italian companies over the years. Before confirming the kidnappings, Italian investigators started watching anyone and everyone who might be tied to

Libyan interests, the Camorra or radical Islam. Di Leva and his wife topped all the lists.

Once the news of the kidnapping broke, Di Leva sent a nonchalant WhatsApp message to his wife to see if she had heard. She was apparently well aware, writing back: "Already done, old news, I'm already in touch. They have those from where we went . . . I'm already working with calm and caution." Police were intrigued, to say the least. Through covert surveillance and undercover officers working both in Libya and in Camorra circles, they tightened the noose around the couple, arresting them in a giant sting operation near Naples. They lived on the upper floors of a building they owned and rented out the lower level to a Moroccan man who runs the Sheìk Narghile Arabian Bar and Restaurant, which advertises nightly belly dancing and Moroccan food, neither of which are particularly popular with Nigerians or Neapolitans, but which were apparently quite popular among those with whom the couple associated. In their living room, they displayed a photo of themselves together with Iranian President Mahmoud Ahmadinejad.

After their arrest, their email accounts offered a window into an established enterprise with lucrative business deals across the Middle East and North Africa, including countries where ISIS fighters are present, for weapons put together in Italy and shipped back out of the port of Naples illegally. The money was allegedly laundered through their son's accounts both in Italy and abroad, and they conducted business with the sort of blatant confidence of a crime family, knowing that they might be under surveillance, but never too worried about actually getting caught.

Messages from middlemen and buyers were friendly, implying close relationships. Some were one-line notes asking for urgent delivery of Sam-7 surface-to-air missiles and Soviet-made weaponry. Other messages contained veritable grocery lists for munitions and even souped-up helicopters.

Catello Maresca, head of the Naples anti-Mafia and anti-terrorism unit, says his team was able to connect the couple to weapons and helicopters intended for ISIS fighters in Libya, including nearly fourteen thousand M14 semi-automatic rifles, a military air ambulance that was converted for assault use, MI-17 Soviet assault helicopters, and at least three Italian A129 Mongoose attack helicopters. Some of the weapons intended for Iran never left the port of Naples because of a logistics mix-up; investigators say the defendants are still charged with trafficking the entire inventory because of their intent and the overall *malaffare* in which they were involved.

The investigation into their arms trade uncovered strong ties to Francesco Chianese, a fruit vendor and Camorra associate who was arrested in 2015 for arms trafficking to known jihadi fighters under police surveillance. The cops weren't concerned that the group was planning attacks here, but they were sure they were using Italy as a crucial corridor to move weapons to those who might have such intentions in other European countries. Chianese, who was referred to as "O Santulillo," had spent time training militias in Libya and Nigeria and was well known to the Nigerian gangs in Castel Volturno as a trusted intermediary. Anti-terrorism investigators in the northern Veneto region had first heard of Chianese while investigating an emerging extremist cell with ties to a jihadi cell in France. Much of the information from the ongoing investigation remains sealed, no doubt to avoid tipping off others involved in the racket, but what is known is that Chianese's business was dependent on arms parts that were smuggled into the port of Naples inside extra-large Nigerian potatoes – a curious import to Italy to say the least.

Di Leva's wife is thought to have been the mastermind of the arms trafficking operation, acting as a goodwill ambassador between the weapons buyers in other countries and the sellers in Italy. She and her husband had set up shell companies in Ukraine and kept bank accounts in Panama, according to the investigators working on unraveling their extensive network.

The middle-aged arms traders are not unique in the Land of Fires. In November 2015, not long after the Paris attacks, Italian police carried out several raids against suspected Camorra weapons traffickers they believed were supplying arms to terrorist cells in Europe. They also found evidence that the Camorra was helping terrorist groups recruit mercenaries, both by offering them protection once they were in the country and by providing safe passage into Europe.[59] They reportedly offered terrorist recruits short-term black-market employment in illicit drugs and arms sales to help them raise money to carry out their plans. Italy's anti-Mafia unit fears that some southern Italians are even taken by the ISIS ideology, noting that many young men in the hinterland around Naples have started wearing beards and are, as far as they can tell, supporters of Islamic State ideology.

TERRORISM

Time and again, investigations into the collaboration between the Camorra and international terrorism lead directly to the Nigerian criminal gangs, who provide a crucial link as middle-men between the two sides. Anis Amri, the ISIS-inspired perpetrator of the 2016 Berlin Christmas Market massacre, who came to Italy by way of Lampedusa in 2011, was overheard by German counter-terrorism authorities promising associates that he could easily procure Kalashnikovs from his "black friends" in Naples for reasonable prices "to fight for our faith at any cost." The German authorities had heard the same claims about getting weapons in Naples so many times before that it didn't even raise a red flag.

"Naples has been, for many years, a central logistics base for the Middle East," Franco Roberti, the prominent anti-Mafia prosecutor, told me in an interview in 2016. "The Camorra is also active in the world of jihadist terrorism that passes through

Naples. [The city] lends itself to this type of activity. In the past there have been contacts between jihadi militants and the Camorra clans."

Whether the local authorities can't or won't stop the illicit arms activity is debatable. But it is especially worrying that the criminality has been linked to Islamic State sympathizers who are trying to enter Europe by posing as refugees.[60] Concerns that potential terrorists are hiding among the legitimate refugees and economic migrants has been a battle cry for far-right and other anti-immigration groups for years, and it's an argument that bears hearing out.

In May 2016, CNN interviewed a human smuggler named Abu Walid in Tripoli, Libya, who said he had been asked by an Islamic State operative to transport twenty-five fighters on his next boat to Italy.[61] The pay wasn't exceptional, just $40,000 for all twenty-five men, which boils down to $1,600 a head – about a quarter of what Walid and others who run migrant ships usually charge. Walid said no, not out of integrity or concern for the safety of Europeans, but so that he could fill his boat with higher-paying migrants and desperate refugees and trafficked women. He had no idea whether the ISIS fighter found another smuggler to transport his sinister human cargo.

Many of the male migrants and refugees who come over by sea and who find themselves caught up in criminal activities like drug dealing end up in Italian prisons, which are known incubators for radical extremism. Italian authorities have their eye on more than four hundred men who, like Berlin killer Amri, have been radicalized by incarcerated Islamic State sympathizers. Italy's Justice Minister Andrea Orlando says Italy's overcrowded prisons, like the one in Palermo in which Amri spent four years, are "hotbeds for radicalization."

More than 160 people with suspected ties to Islamic extremism were expelled from Italy between 2015 and 2017. They include a number of people kept under surveillance in prison and a handful of Amri's associates, including several who lived in a house in the town of Latina, north of Castel Volturno. When he was shot and killed in Milan, Amri had a cellphone with the numbers of some of his old inmate friends who were added to various watch lists, though few have undergone any formal investigations. It is not illegal to be in possession of ISIS propaganda in Italy, so even if they did have it on their phones, as Amri did, it wouldn't be enough necessarily to kick them out. Only in the cases where those being expelled are taken back by their countries of origin, usually at those countries' expense, can Italians be sure the suspected terrorists are gone. But often, as was the case when Amri was freed, no one checks if they actually leave. And if they do leave, there's nothing to stop them simply turning around and coming right back.

Amri's obvious ties to radical extremism did prompt Italian officials to pay more attention to what's going on in prisons, and in early 2017, they started tapping calls between a Tunisian inmate named Saber Hmidi and his wife after suspecting that he was recruiting potential Islamic State fighters whom he planned to join in Syria on his release. He had also spent time in the same prison as Amri and the two knew each other. On the phone, his Italian wife warned him that he was changing. She became so concerned that she told friends she felt he might do something terrible. He was apparently radicalized after a brief incarceration on drug charges tied to work he had picked up with the Camorra. He was only out for a few months when he pulled a gun on two police officers, which landed him a second, longer sentence and led some to question whether he wanted to go back to prison to continue his recruitment. Because of Italy's dire overcrowding situation in its prisons, he was moved around between facilities for administrative reasons. Each time he was in a new prison, he allegedly was able to gather a group of aspiring terrorists to preach to. Authorities put Saber in maximum security while they attempted to unravel his extensive web.

FALSE DOCUMENTS AND MONEY

An integral component of the illegal sex, drugs and arms trades is the need for falsified documents, whether they are fake pro forma customs forms or biometric passports. The Camorra's machinery licenses are easily fudged and so are the permits that allow import and export through the Neapolitan ports. The use of false documents is especially important in the trafficking of humans, notably for those who end up in sex slavery.

Blessing's visa, for instance, was legitimately affiliated with her passport, even though it was given for work at a false company. The Nigerian authorities initially caught the problem until her sponsor Alice either paid them off or worked out a deal with them, but it easily passed a basic inspection by border guards in Spain because it was not machine readable.

Between 2013 and 2015, thousands of blank Italian identity cards with official seals that were ready to be completed with photos and personal details were stolen from municipal offices in and around Caserta. The thefts worried law enforcement officials across Europe because the cards would allow whoever had them to travel unchecked throughout the twenty-six border-free Schengen states in Europe. Some of the cards were randomly traceable, which is a practice utilized in all European countries in case thefts of this nature occur. They found that many cards had been sold for between €150 and €500 to Syrians and Palestinians who wanted to live in Europe, and to Italians and other Europeans who wanted to go to the Middle East under a false name.

False documents are, in many ways, the glue that holds all these criminal rackets together. Many of the Nigerians who live in Castel Volturno have documents that appear legitimate when traced, despite the fact that the national statistics show less than five percent of migrants from Nigeria have ever been granted any level of asylum or protection. Sub-Saharan Africans generally do not qualify for work visas in Italy outside the diplomatic sector, such as the United Nations, in part due to Italy's high level of unemployment. The numbers don't add up, but when police in Castel Volturno run someone's residency permit through the national system, it usually checks out, despite the assumption that it has been falsified.

In 2017, Italy's agency for information and external security, known as AISE, stumbled on a fairly banal advertisement in the deep web (the unindexed section of the World Wide Web that can only be accessed through specialized browsers). It traced the advert to a Neapolitan firm promising biometric British passports for around €2,000 or 4.113 Bitcoin.[62] The website looked very professional and included a photo of the British passport seal, yet the advertisement made no secret of its criminal intent: "We are selling original UK Passports made with your info/picture. Also, your info will get entered into the official passport database. So it's possible to travel with our passports. How do we do it? Trade secret! Information on how to send us your info and picture will be given after purchase! You can even enter the UK/EU with our passports; we can just add a stamp for the country you are in. Ideal for people who want to work in the EU/UK."

Police believe the deep web advertisements might be connected to a man who operates under the name "Amponsah," who they believe runs a little laboratory somewhere around Caserta about half-way between Naples and Castel Volturno where he makes passports, identity cards and visas. He's also able to hack into the national register so that when police check the documents, they appear valid. His work is well known, but his whereabouts have been elusive so far.

Many times, as in Blessing's case, these false documents are sent first to the Italian embassy in Nigeria either so that people can fly to Italy rather than take the rickety boats, or so that they won't have problems once they get to the country. The fact that a false document like a visa could end up in a legitimate passport implies widespread complicity between people working in the embassies, but there has been little effort to explore that route of investigation. Nigeria's government is notoriously corrupt, consistently ranking among the top forty of the most corrupt countries in the world, with a score of twenty-eight out of a hundred. (For comparison, the UK scores eighty-one, and is the tenth 'cleanest' country in the world according to this index.)[63]

Italians have been proven to be easily corruptible, too, scoring forty-seven out of a hundred on the Transparency International corruption index, so it is hard to know where to begin to break the cycle.

Blessing believes that people in both countries worked to secure her fake visa, which was tied to a business that clearly did not exist. Such cooperation would likely negate the effect of any safeguards to protect women from trafficking. It's hard to find a red flag in a complicit system.

The Camorra also needs non-traceable money to operate its varied enterprises. Sometimes they just make it themselves. The town of Giugliano, between Caserta and Castel Volturno, is considered the counterfeit capital of Europe. The European Central Bank says more than half of the euro notes taken out of circulation as counterfeit each year come from Giugliano, but in terms of annual income, counterfeiting falls far short of the document, drugs and sex trades. More often, the Camorra's liquid operating funds come from protection money, including the hefty fee Nigerian gangs have to pay to operate their drug trade. The Nigerian gangs, of course, make that money quite literally off the backs of the sex slaves.

TERRORISM TIES IN EUROPE

Italian anti-Mafia and counter-terrorism police are on a constant hunt for points at which organized crime and terrorist activities intersect. Since the 9/11 attacks in the United States, Italy's anti-Mafia police have been warning the authorities in America and other countries that it will only be a matter of time before international terrorists join forces with the Mafia.

United States security cables exposed through WikiLeaks paint a picture of great concern. According to a cable dated 6 June 2008, "the Italian crime syndicates help support terrorist groups in Colombia and Central Asia through drug trafficking; violate the intellectual property rights of American businesses and artists; buttress organized crime in the United States; pose potential public health risks to US military and dependents stationed in southern Italy; and weaken an important ally."[64]

European terror attacks in France, Belgium, Germany and the United Kingdom in the past five years have all involved at least one person tied in some way to Italy, whether they entered the country illegally as a refugee or took advantage of the Mafia's network of fake documents, drugs and arms.

At least two of the November 2015 Paris suicide attackers were in possession of false documents originating from Italy, according to the Italian investigation that led to the arrest of a Moroccan man named Mohamed Lahlaoui.[65] The 28-year-old was arrested on terrorism charges in Germany in March 2016. He had been given a deportation notice to leave the northern Italian city of Brescia in May 2014 after he failed to check in with his probation officer after being convicted of attempted murder and weapons and drugs trafficking charges.

No one kept track of him after he was told to leave Italy and he wasn't given a second thought until he was stopped in Germany. His name wasn't on any terror list, but the police asked to see his cellphone after he started acting suspiciously. Their hunch was right. What they found was a message from Khalid El Bakraoui, one of the suicide-bomber brothers who blew up twenty passengers in a Brussels subway a few days earlier. The message was sent at 9:08 A.M., just three minutes before the bomb went off. It said, simply, "*fin*" – French for "the end."

Authorities were sure that Lahlaoui may have also been friends with other attackers, including Salah Abdeslam, the terrorist driver tied to both the Brussels airport and subway attacks and the Paris attacks in 2015, who had evaded authorities for four months. What was of particular note to police was that Bakraoui traveled through Italy on a budget Ryanair flight the day before Abdeslam arrived by ferry into the southern port of Bari. Abdeslam ended up driving north and his trail was lost after he used a credit card at a highway tollbooth. Lahlaoui was back in Brussels a month later where he was treated for knife wounds in a Belgian emergency room the same day Abdeslam was arrested in a hail of bullets in a raid in Brussels.

Authorities in Italy eventually also tied Lahlaoui to Djamal Eddine Ouali, a forty-year-old Algerian picked up in Salerno in March 2016 on charges that he supplied fake documents to the Brussels subway bombers and many others.

Lahlaoui might have also been linked to Anas El Abboubi, a jihadi rapper featured on an ISIS recruitment video who admits to being radicalized as a youth and whose name features on a list of 22,000 Islamic State fighter recruits.[66] The two attended the same Islamic culture center and lived just a few miles apart, near Brescia. Abboubi is the mastermind behind the Sharia4Italia recruitment website, which authorities say is responsible for the recruitment of hundreds of foreign fighters in Italy, many of whom eventually go to Syria to fight.

One of the men who paid special attention to Abboubi's work was Youssef Zaghba, a twenty-two-year-old Italian-Moroccan terrorist who was part of a trio of men who drove a van into pedestrians on London Bridge before being killed in June 2017. I interviewed Zaghba's mother in her modest apartment near Bologna shortly after her son's identity was released.[67] She told me he was radicalized on the internet and was a fan of Abboubi's music. She had even seen him on the Sharia4Italia website.

Authorities started trailing Abboubi in 2012, after he gave an interview to MTV about music and Islam, in which he expressed his radical views. They finally arrested him a year later after discovering a plan to blow up a busy shopping area in Brescia.

For unknown reasons, no doubt related to Italy's dysfunctional court system, Abboubi was released while awaiting trial. He escaped to Syria, where he changed his name to Anas al-Italy and continued to post on Sharia4Italia and Facebook until 2015. The same year, Zaghba was stopped at the airport in Bologna as he tried to board a one-way flight to Turkey with the intent to join the fight in Syria. He told investigators at the time that he was going to be a terrorist, mistaking the Italian word for tourist, which is similar. "It was his conscience talking," his mother told me. "It's what he really meant." Stopped from going to Syria to fight, Zaghba traveled to London on his Italian passport where his mother says he worked in a fast-food chicken restaurant with other young men she didn't like. "He was stopped [from] going to Syria," his mother said, "so he found another way."

Despite having so many ties to recent terror attacks, Italy has not been targeted like other European cities, though ISIS operatives consistently threaten Rome and the Vatican in their propaganda. Historically, organized crime in Italy always wins, if not in the eyes of the law, then at least in practice on the streets. How much longer that keeps Italy safe from a terrorist attack is a big question. Italian authorities will argue that the reason Italy has stayed safe is because of their police work, which was perfected through years of national terrorism by the Red Brigades during the seventies and eighties and has remained strong due to the country's constant battle with organized crime. Legal wiretapping, surveillance and general eavesdropping require little more than a judge's signature, and often not even that, and are carried out with great frequency, used to thwart plans or expel potential terrorists. That heavy surveillance may keep Italy relatively safe, but it also underscores how much the Italian authorities know and choose to ignore in other criminal sectors. If they are able to gather enough intelligence to thwart terror attacks, why can't they do more about drugs, arms and sex trafficking?

Migrants and refugees march in Rome to demand
better treatment and protection.

7

THE WAY FORWARD

"It's not like I'm having an affair. That would be cheating." – "Giovanni," client along the Via Domitiana

ALONG THE VIA DOMITIANA – Giovanni drives his white Fiat Uno up and down the Domitiana, window-shopping for sex almost every Sunday morning while his wife thinks that he's at church. Giovanni's ruse is an excuse for him to take a shower and put on aftershave without making her suspicious. By his own admission, his goal is to experience a blowjob by as many different Nigerian women as he can because, in his words, the "dirtiness of having a black woman's mouth on him" is a turn on. Plus, if he never goes to the same woman twice, he can never be accused of having a relationship outside of his marriage. If he errs and accidentally stops his Fiat beside the same woman two Sundays in a row, he says he apologizes and moves on.

Giovanni is a short, balding man with a thick neck full of gray stubble and a potbelly that flops over the top of his trousers, which could easily describe half the Italians who live in and around Castel Volturno. He is around fifty-five years old and runs one of the little shops along the Domitiana. He dotes on his wife, calling her *amore* (love) and *tesoro* (treasure) as she minds the till, and seems like the last person in the world who would frequent the girls on the street.

I discovered that Giovanni was a client by accident when I was looking for someone to explain to me just who the patrons of the many women standing on the Domitiana really are.

Because he was a local, I thought he would know about them; I really didn't suspect he was one.

I often stopped at their business whenever I was on a reporting trip as they had an exceptionally clean bathroom, which is a rare treat anywhere around Castel Volturno. I had been there several times before I finally asked his wife about the clients who go to the girls lined up on either side of their shop. She gave a sideways look at her husband standing behind the deli counter and shrugged.

"*No lo so*," she whispered. "I don't know."

I then asked Giovanni, who pondered my question. After a few minutes, he told me to come back later that afternoon when he reopened at four o'clock after his siesta break. He would try to have someone come to the shop who could help me with my questions.

When I returned, he was there alone. He said his wife was at home with their children. He was not at all embarrassed and extremely candid about paying for sex. It seemed almost natural to him and, as is often the case when it comes to discussing sex with Italian men, he was not reluctant at all to talk in what turned out to be quite explicit detail about it. While in no way do I wish to protect the clients who keep this lurid business of sex slavery alive, I promised Giovanni, which is not his real name, relative anonymity if he was honest with me about being a long-time client. I keep that promise out of respect for his wife and their children.

He said his first experience with a prostitute was when he was eighteen years old and stationed outside of Pisa, doing what used to be mandatory military service, which was discontinued in 2005. Many Italian men were first introduced to paying for sex during this time; apparently it was an open tradition that went back many generations. Both before and after World War II, it was a highly accepted rite of passage for Italian men to lose their virginity at brothels, which were regulated by the state until 1958, at which point Italy deregulated sex work but kept prostitution legal. It was frowned upon by the Catholic Church for young women to lose their virginity before marriage, so it was accepted that the boys had no other choice. Usually their fathers and uncles would take them, or, alternatively, they would wait for military service and go in groups.

Giovanni described weekend furloughs from the military academy when he and the other cadets would go into Pisa to find mostly Eastern European prostitutes who would hand them a condom, lift up their skirts and bend over in the dark back alleys behind the Leaning Tower of Pisa for five to ten euro. He said dozens of service men, all around eighteen or nineteen years old, would simply line up, drinking beer between blowjobs and quickie sex. He saw nothing wrong with it. "How else do you learn?" he asked. "No one wants an Italian woman who is a whore, so what are the options?"

That said, Giovanni did not lose his virginity to a prostitute. He had lost his confidence after the first time he had had sex with an Italian girlfriend and says that the prostitutes in Pisa "cured him." By his account, he went dozens, maybe fifty or more times, during his year of military service. "Once a weekend," he said.

Then, when he returned to Castel Volturno, he met the woman who would eventually be his wife. They had a healthy sex life and two children, plus a late-term miscarriage. He says he refrained from frequenting the girls on the streets during most of his early marriage, but occasionally during each pregnancy he "gave in to temptation once or twice."

In 2006, his wife was in a car accident in Naples that left her with a fractured spine, which made sex terribly painful for her, so he eventually stopped asking. He said that he never had intercourse with the Nigerian women and that he felt that fellatio did not count as betrayal. "It's not in the Bible," he said.

He suspects his wife knows about his encounters, but that she would surely forgive him because, as he says, "she can no longer please me." In retrospect, I should have asked if his wife ever performed fellatio on him, or if he still tried to satisfy her orally or in any other way.

"What does she expect me to do? It's not like I'm having an affair. That would be cheating," he says. "Paying the whores is not an affair."

I asked if the constant availability of so many women on the streets made it easy for him. "You mean like a fat man living in a candy store? Sure," he said. "If someone tries to sell you something you are missing every time you pass by, eventually you are going to give in and buy it."

He didn't seem at all bothered that many of the women were kept on the street against their will. "No one will hire them to do any other work," he shrugged. "If they want to live in this country, they've got to do something for society." He seemed even less bothered about Camorra involvement in the Nigerian racket, reminding me of the 2008 massacre at the Ob Ob Exotic Fashions tailor shop and the fact that the Camorra and Nigerians were partners.

"They all work together to make money," he said. "There is no other way here."

Many women on the frontline of the sex trafficking crisis believe that prostitution should be made illegal in Italy to combat the exploitation of Nigerian women and others, but not everyone agrees that it would stop the problem. If prostitution were illegal, there would easily still be sex trafficking. Criminalizing it would take vital work away from thousands of sex workers who, however coerced, choose prostitution to support themselves and their families. By some estimates, more than half of the Nigerian women who finally pay off their madams stay on the streets as legitimate prostitutes, free from debt bondage. Even some of those who are rescued from sex trafficking eventually return to the street out of financial desperation. When a girl has been conditioned to believe that her only option is to sell her body, she often starts believing it.

Others argue that regulating sex work could be beneficial,

even though allowing the existence of brothels might actually make identifying trafficked women even harder, precisely because they would no longer have to be out on the streets. The reality is, however, that most Nigerian trafficked women already work in brothel-like conditions, like the connection houses in Castel Volturno and the rat-infested street-level apartments in Palermo. Legalizing brothels likely wouldn't have any impact on their madams' business models and methods because the madams surely wouldn't be able to open legitimate brothels without the risk of being found out as traffickers. One benefit such regulation might have would be to put more pressure on clients, because they, too, would potentially have to register to go to brothels, although it's unlikely any of these rules would ever apply in a place like Castel Volturno. The priority, there-fore, should be to adopt measures that would provide a means by which trafficked women can be identified *before* they get on the street, not after.

IOM and other advocacy programs are instead aimed at educating clients like Giovanni, who may be oblivious to the true nature of "what they are purchasing." The IOM's Carlotta Santarossa, would like to see a system in place that tries to break through that barrier of ignorance in the sex market. "They should know that with the sex, they are buying a woman who has been raped and abused," she says. "The men should know they are facilitating more misery."

The lack of will to hold clients accountable or regulate sex work most certainly comes from the fact that many lawmakers are themselves clients. Even Silvio Berlusconi, the thrice-elected and longest serving prime minister the country has ever had, was convicted of abetting underage prostitution with a young Moroccan woman known as "Ruby the Heartstealer."[68] He was acquitted in an appellate trial when his lawyers success-fully proved he didn't know her age. Piero Marrazzo, the gover-nor of Lazio, Rome's home region, was caught with a trans-prostitute, which is not illegal, but because he was married and the trans-prostitute, known as Brenda, was later found dead in her apartment, he lost his job over the incident. He has since returned to the political arena.

The only deterrent that has successfully curbed the appetite for the sex trafficked women, however marginally, is shaming the clients into not stopping on the roadside. Castel Volturno's mayor Dimitri Russo is a criminal lawyer who has tried almost everything to stop the racket. In 2013, his city council finally came up with an ingenious plan to institute a loitering ordinance that makes it illegal to stop anywhere on the Domitiana that is not a licensed place of business. He coerced two of his councilwomen to dress as sex workers and try to solicit clients while he hid behind a fence. When the clients stopped, he ran out to the cars wearing the standard green, white and red mayoral sash all Italian officials wear when on official duty and handed out pamphlets that gave instructions about safe sex and human trafficking. A television crew filmed each encounter with a would-be John from behind a hidden fence.

The cars all sped away, but not before a complicit police officer waiting down the road stopped them and fined them under the no loitering ordinance. They all paid the fine immediately, pleading with the police not to deliver the ticket to their homes. The campaign lasted only a few days and was highly publicized, but did little to stop the clients on a long-term basis, even though much of the footage was aired on local TV and remains on YouTube.

A few months later, a different local police officer in Castel Volturno tried a similar strategy to shame the men who picked up the girls by taking a picture of their cars as the women got into the fronts seats. He then traced the license plates and summoned the drivers to the police station, where he slapped the no-loitering fine on them and showed them the pictures. Again, though, the campaign had little long-term impact.

Around the same time the officer with the camera was out,

police started monitoring a trio of hotels along the Domitiana. Hotel Tiuna, l'Hotel Millennium and Hotel Le Dune had become alternative service rooms when the connection houses run by the madams were full. Girls were given keys for designated rooms that had been paid for in advance where they could bring clients they picked up on the streets. Eventually, the hotel owners decided that they could also make money off the women, so they allegedly started allowing them to work directly out of the hotel without having to solicit men from the streets. According to court documents, full floors were designated to sex workers where men knew they could essentially shop door-to-door for a woman they liked, each charging between twenty to twenty-five euro a client. The price was higher than that charged on the street because the hotel also took a cut.

Just thirteen people, including a handful of frequent clients as well as the owners of the hotels, were arrested in a sting operation in mid-2016. Many of the women and clients who would have normally been there were warned in advance about the arrest. Even though brothels are illegal, the clients were ultimately arrested for not legally registering at the hotels, which is required by law in Italy due to anti-Mafia legislation that is meant to be an obstacle for mob-owned hotels wanting to harbor fugitives. It also meant that none of the clients would be charged with anything to do with prostitution.

Protecting the clients' identity is clearly part of the problem in sex trafficking. The thinking is that if the clients could also be held accountable, they could actually help save trafficked women. When Blessing was forced to sell sex, she cried out to each and every man who stopped to be with her, pleading with them that she didn't want to have sex and that instead she wanted to be saved. Only one client in her four days on the street agreed not to have sex with her. The rest forced themselves upon her despite her pleas that she did not want to have sex with them. Some forced her to perform oral sex. Others essentially raped her.

So far, no legislation is even being drawn up that would

address the issue of holding clients accountable, despite groups like IOM and other anti-trafficking entities insisting that laws must change in this regard.

Placing the blame squarely on the clients' shoulders obviously oversimplifies the problem. With so many women already in Italy it is hard to imagine that, even if the clients cooperated in identifying trafficked women, they wouldn't be exploited in other ways. They would surely be made to work in underground brothels or as drug mules or even sold as laborers. Perhaps their organs would be harvested. In 2016, an Eritrean trafficker named Atta Wehabrebi gave testimony in exchange for protection against prosecution, telling Italian investigators that migrants who couldn't afford to pay for their journeys were forced to sell their organs to an Egyptian criminal ring.[69] Others who were kidnapped were killed for their organs, which were sold to Russians and wealthy Eastern Europeans who didn't want to die on organ donor waiting lists. In 2015, several bodies washed up on the shores near Alexandria, Egypt, with cuts where their organs had been surgically removed.[70] It is easy to envision that any number of rackets would develop to continue to exploit the girls until something changes within Italian society and its culture of looking the other way.

Sometimes clients see themselves as the girls' saviors. Giovanni, for one, insists that he is always clean and gentle with the women, which he says he is sure is not always the case. There are also legendary stories in Castel Volturno about clients falling in love with the women, including some who are able to persuade the girls to leave the streets, often paying off their debts to their madams to secure their freedom.

But make no mistake, the clients are seldom the heroes in this tragedy.

In 2016, Antonio Matarazzo, a seventy-five-year-old retired farmer from Calabria, was arrested for beating one of the Nigerian women on the Domitiana with his pistol after she refused to continue what he thought was a real relationship. He had been hiring her for sex for several years and had apparently fallen in love with her. When she refused to come with him out of fear her madam would find and kill her, however, he grew jealous and started stalking her and the various clients she picked up, sometimes butting their cars with his, according to the police report of his arrest. Her madam told her to get rid of the old man, so she refused to see him anymore. Her friends watched as he dragged her into his car one night and nearly beat her to death before leaving her bleeding on the street. Eventually she was taken to the emergency room in Castel Volturno, where she almost died in surgery. Police caught up with Matarazzo as he was driving back to Calabria, the bloody pistol still on the front seat of his car. He pleaded a crime of passion and, because of his age, was never sentenced to jail time for the assault.

The truth is, clients who frequent the sex trafficked women generally make no distinction between them and legitimate prostitutes on the street, which makes them hard to profile. Even the women who have been forced into sex slavery tend not to be able to paint a general picture of the local clients beyond describing them as "hairy" compared to African men. There are few studies on the matter, but one about clients of prostitutes in Italy conducted by the Abele Group in Turin a few years ago found that seventy percent of the estimated 2.5 million Italian men who regularly frequent prostitutes are married.[71] The number of overall clients is based on a dubious formula assuming that around thirty thousand legitimate prostitutes turn ten different tricks a day, seven days a week. The study showed that the most sought-after prostitute was black, preferably around sixteen years old, though it failed to address sex-trafficked women, which are thought to number more than thirty thousand in Italy alone. The average turnover for those in Castel Volturno is up to fifteen or even twenty clients a day, because they are forced to work longer hours to pay off their fictitious debts.

In observing cars stopping to chat or pick up girls along the

Domitiana, a type definitely emerges. Whether they drive a BMW or a delivery truck, most of the men tend to look at least like they are past their fifties, often bald or with gray hair. Because they don't get out of the cars themselves, it is difficult to estimate whether most are thin or fat. Some are clearly wealthy, based on their cars and sunglasses. Others are clearly not. Some men stop on motorcycles. The teenage boys who stop are invariably riding mopeds.

Women are rarely clients, though there are exceptions and some do stop for a lesbian experience, according to many of the girls I have interviewed. Some of the Nigerian women agree to it if they can get by with charging more. More often, women are part of a couple looking for a threesome. Many of the girls on the street will concede, not least of all because they do charge extra for group sex. A common complaint is that "the Italian women are very mean." Some want to watch their boyfriends or husbands having domineering or degrading sex with a black woman, sometimes even tying them up or filming the encounter. Sometimes the girls are paid to give hand jobs or perform fellatio on the men while the women take pictures or videos for the man's later viewing.

A few priests, too, are known to be regular clients, according to many of the girls I have interviewed, who say they are among the nicer men. So are American soldiers who are stationed at the nearby military installments and NATO bases, who the women say tend to be "cleaner" and are often circumcised, unlike European men, and less inclined to demand more degrading acts such as forced anal sex. Finally, there are the groups of "sex tourists" who travel to the area from all over Europe for "whore weekends." These men also tend to be heavy drug users, which makes them either violent or docile. One of the Nigerian women I interviewed said she and another Nigerian woman were each regularly paid several hundred euros to spend the weekend in a hotel room and have two-on-one sex with Russian or German men who lined up at the door to wait their turns. While hardly enjoyable, she said it was much better than standing out on the street, not least of all because they asked the men to shower before touching them. Men who pick up the girls on the streets are rarely clean.

Many of the young women at Casa Ruth and those who still work the streets point to a growing trend toward teenage boys as clients. Some have been introduced to sex through online pornography and, in the absence of a girl their age who might allow them to experiment, feel that they can do as they please with the women who work the streets.

The biggest difference between the middle-aged men who make up the bulk of the clientele and the teenagers, they say, is that the younger clients are more likely to use condoms, whereas the older ones rarely do. Giovanni said that he had never once put on a condom for a blowjob, despite the risk of sexually transmitted diseases, implying that women on the streets only insist on them for intercourse.

Sister Rita blames the clients entirely for the whole prostitution racket. If not for them, she believes, the Camorra and Nigerian gangs would have to find other means to make money for their illicit trades and sex trafficking would die out. She feels that the clients get a free pass from authorities and that everyone excuses their behavior because Italy accepts that men are both patriarchal and philanderers. "Even the wives know," she says. "If we punished the men, these women would be free."

It is hard even to fathom what would happen in a place like Castel Volturno if sex trafficking or any of the criminality was suddenly stopped and the girls were free. They have no documents, no money and the outright denial and lack of public support about how to improve the lives of trafficked women would surely prove an insurmountable challenge. The success in helping the few women who are rescued depends, in large part, on making them independent. Regular Italian unemployment, however, remains at around twelve percent, with youth unemployment at thirty-five percent. If Italians can't get jobs, surely undocumented Nigerians have no chance. The "work no one wants to do," which tends to be babysitting and house-cleaning, is largely taken up by Italy's large Filipino community and the *badante* or elderly care market tends to go to Romanians.

In an effort to keep women who have been rescued off the streets, most agencies and cooperatives that work to rescue trafficked women just start their own businesses and employ the people they are helping that way. But even then they rarely make ends meet and the women can almost never make enough to support themselves. The danger, of course, is that, when they can't afford basic amenities, they will return to the one money-making scheme they know out of desperation.

To try to combat this, Casa Ruth opened up its small coop-erative factory a few years ago where the women can make African handicrafts that they then sell in a small boutique near the church in downtown Caserta.[72] They buy bright, colorful material straight from a supplier in Senegal or through distribu-tors in Holland, and have been able to collect half a dozen old Singer sewing machines, which are now lined up on makeshift plywood tables in a building that once housed a funeral parlor.

The women work in the factory for a few hours a day and split the profits from the sale of the crafts, which include party favors, potholders, aprons and notebook covers. Still, few can survive without additional help. I had a heated conversation with Blessing one afternoon in which she said that the traf-ficked women aren't looking for handouts. "If one more person offers me their old clothes, I'll scream," she said. "Give me a job, give me a chance, don't give me the old things you don't want."

Dozens of other entities exist solely because of the *malaffare* that permeates the area due to the drug and sex trafficking rack-ets. Emergency is an Italian non-governmental organization that operates primarily in warzones like Libya, Iraq and Afghanistan, providing free medical aid to those in need.[73] In

2013, they sent a mobile clinic to Castel Volturno, where they found that Nigerians living in squalor were consistently denied access to state-run health care, in part because they didn't have transportation to take them to area hospitals or clinics.

Two years later, unable to keep up with the demand with their mobile clinic, they opened a fixed emergency room on the Domitiana. They have since set up similar clinics in Sicily, where a huge number of asylum seekers and irregular migrants live in the periphery. "Day after day, we've been able to see for ourselves all the problems linked with access to treatment in a place where the issues of urban decay are compounded by the well-rooted presence of organized crime," their Italian director Cecilia Strada says about opening a clinic in Castel Volturno, noting that their mission statement is still focused on serving people in conflict zones generally associated with war, which she says Castel Volturno is in many ways.

What is perhaps most remarkable about the sheer desperation along the Domitiana is the presence of hope among the survivors of this horrific life. In November 2008, South African singer Miriam Makeba, better known as Mama Africa, took to the stage in Castel Volturno for a unity concert in honor of those who had lost their lives in the Ob Ob Exotic Fashions tailor shop massacre. It wasn't so much the scope of the tragedy in terms of the number of dead, but the message it sent that the Camorra had killed African migrants over turf they illegally control. It was billed as an anti-Mafia event that also paid homage to Roberto Saviano, who at the time was just emerging as a fearless hero for his investigative work against the Mafia. The stage was set on Baia Verde, not far from the abandoned edifices of the Coppola Village, and there was a sense of reluctant hope in the air for the first time in months.

Makeba spent thirty-one years in exile in the United States after South African authorities revoked her passport in an effort to extinguish her voice of resistance against apartheid. It did little to silence her. She testified against the South African government at a special United Nations session in 1963 and she spoke and wrote and sang about the racial injustices in her country throughout her celebrated career. In North America, she achieved enviable fame, known for introducing authentic African music to popular musicians of the time. She toured with Harry Belafonte and even sang at one of President John F. Kennedy's lavish birthday parties. She was also the first African to win a Grammy.

Makeba offered the perfect ray of hope and a voice of reason to the fractured community of Castel Volturno, still shaken by the murders and subsequent riots less than two months earlier. She was a trusted unifier who had lived through and seen the struggles between blacks and whites first hand. People trusted her. Plus, she brought a touch of celebrity to an area seemingly long written off as a hotbed for corruption. The event felt important, but politicians and dignitaries outnumbered the African community by two to one. The army was still patrolling the streets after the Ob Ob Exotic Fashions tailor shop massacre and most who stayed home did so out of a justifiable fear that the event was just a trap to round them up and deport them.

The Castel Volturno gig was one of a chosen few appearances for the ageing musician, who was on a farewell tour after announcing her retirement in 2005. Getting her on the playbill in Castel Volturno was a coup for the concert organizers and the evening was one of celebration, music and, for the first time in the complicated history of Castel Volturno, recognition that something needed to be done to help the divided community make peace.

Then everything went wrong.

In what was a poignantly symbolic last act of the night, Makeba finished her set with her famous song "Pata Pata," a global radio hit that got the crowd singing and dancing. Then she took a bow, walked off stage and collapsed. Moments later, she had the first of what would be a series of fatal heart attacks.

Within minutes, the woman who had provided a glimmer of hope to a troubled town was rushed off to the Pineta Grande clinic in a noisy parade of ambulance sirens and police lights that most assumed were surely from yet another act of random violence in the community. Doctors couldn't revive her and she died in Castel Volturno a few hours later, at the age of seventy-six.

As truly tragic as her death was, her legacy lives on in Castel Volturno in ways that it would not have had she simply left the stage and flown back home. There seemed to be a certain symbolism in the icon taking her last breath in such a troubled place. She was the ultimate martyr for racial tensions and she died in a place in which the hope for unity seemed a lost cause.

After her death, the Mondo Senza Confini (World Without Borders) Miriam Makeba Cultural Center was founded on the Domitiana.[74] It has meeting rooms where frequent musical events are held and an area dedicated to African culture, with art and clothing. Money is raised to give scholarships to those Nigerian descendants who want to pursue education elsewhere.

Makeba's life work is celebrated with concerts and special cultural events every year. But even more than that, her death seemed to galvanize the African community to demand rights and recognition, and, though it has been an upward struggle to achieve anything close to equality, the fight hasn't been lost completely. There are young Africans in Castel Volturno who want more than what is their perceived destiny and while there is little representation on the city council or even within the Italian community at large, the parallel culture does try to make its voice heard on issues that are important to them, such as ensuring their children can attend local public schools with native Italians.

Before performing what was her last concert, Makeba spent time at the Fernandes Center, which is something between an emergency room, a refugee reception center and a safe house in an old military barrack.[75] It is a place that every single African in the area knows as somewhere they can always be seen by a doctor, dentist or eye doctor, get a warm meal or spend a safe night no matter what documents they have or what their legal status is. The local doctor at the center is Renato Natale, the former mayor of Casal di Principe who, like the center's director Antonio Casale, is also on the Camorra's hit list. It was fitting that Makeba's last public speech of unity took place there. "When you separate people, they never get to know each other and they learn to suspect each other," she told the gathered crowd a few hours before her last concert. "But when you bring people together, they get to know each other and to know about each other's problems and they find out that we all have the same problems as human beings. Thus we are not afraid of one another."[76]

Director Casale believes that the key to stopping the criminality is giving skills to the Africans who live in Castel Volturno so they have alternatives to the criminal world, though without opportunities, those skills are often wasted. Intensive and situation-based Italian classes and technical courses teaching basic skills are provided for free as a priority to facilitate integration. Fernandes was in place long before the Italian government even recognized the migrant crisis. Now that most of the people who come to Castel Volturno are sucked into the trafficking ring or involved in organized crime, their programs have been adapted to include legal services and counseling for women who try to break away from their madams and the JuJu curse.

One of their more successful programs is a soccer camp that has become something of a recruitment center for various amateur Italian soccer teams who look for standout athletes among the migrants. Many of the young men who arrive in Italy by boat harbor dreams of becoming European soccer stars like Gambia standout Ousman Manneh, who came to Germany by way of Italy as an unaccompanied minor in 2014 and quickly rose through the ranks to become a professional player for Germany's Werder Bremen team.

Some of the soccer inspiration comes from the fact that Naples' professional soccer team Napoli also trains in Castel Volturno, albeit in a heavily guarded exclusive golf club with a sea view that they were able to acquire from the sequestered Coppola property. Three soccer pitches with perfectly groomed natural grass and an exclusive hotel behind tall fences and armed guards are a world away from the rest of Castel Volturno, though the club's captain, Marek Hamšík, from Slovenia, lives in a refurbished apartment on the seaside. No one bothers him, and though he tends to socialize in the much more upscale nearby town of Pozzuoli, he has boosted the community's image in numerous ways.

In what remains a unique opportunity anywhere in Castel Volturno, let alone along the entire migrant trail, Fernandes offers a special program to identify skilled and educated migrants, especially those who have finished high school or university. Blessing is the perfect example of the smallest demographic of trafficked women, often ignored because their needs aren't considered as acute as many others. The vast majority of those arriving by sea don't even have basic math or reading skills. Many of the women I have met can only read numbers to twenty. Some can only write their own names. Illiteracy among migrants is astonishingly high, and most cannot even fill out asylum applications on their own.

Fernandes also helps run the Speranza (hope) Project in conjunction with missionary nuns from the Santa Maria dell Accoglienza reception house. It isn't exactly like Casa Ruth, in part because its location, on the Domitiana itself, makes it almost impossible to keep women who leave the streets safe and hidden. There is also a sense that the nuns at Santa Maria seem somewhat less intuitive than those at Casa Ruth, relying more on God's will that everything will be OK rather than realizing that, according to man's will, everything won't. The sisters at Casa Ruth are every bit as religious, but they are also far more realistic.

Women who escape their madams run a great risk of being kidnapped or killed wherever they find safety, so those who shelter with the nuns at Casa Santa Maria really do have to stay within the confines of the building. Some move on to Casa Ruth if there is space, but most live in what amounts to a prison-like situation until they can get their documents and move on or go back to Nigeria. There are babies here, too, but that doesn't make the house seem any more hopeful.

For all the good the center does, it is under constant scrutiny by law enforcement. In early 2017, two Nigerian men were caught selling heroin to a group of young Neapolitan men at the famed Palazzo Grimaldi, a popular spot for drug trafficking. The Neapolitans escaped and the two Nigerians tried to reach the Fernandes Center. They were caught before entering the gate, and police immediately called for a complete search of the premises. They found nothing, but those who would like to see all Africans deported from Castel Volturno questioned why the men thought they could find safety there and whether or not the center was doing all it could to root out troublemakers.

Still, one of the great benefits of such a long-standing establishment is that it provides a point of reference for the area. It is here that the African NGO known as Cultural Video House, which has offices in Naples, was able to find a pool of amateur actors and do development research in relative safety for a web series they produced called *Connection House*.[77]

The show seeks to expose the drastic problems in Castel Volturno through lighthearted comedy, which they somehow manage to pull off without seeming overly flippant. The premise of the show centers on Lorenzo, the spoiled son of a wealthy Neapolitan businessman who has fallen into difficult times after the family business fails. Lorenzo inherits his grandmother's house in Castel Volturno, which he remembers fondly as a place where he spent summers when the Coppola Village was still swanky.

As it happens, the nonna, or grandmother, takes in a group of undocumented migrants in her later years, including Nigerian women (one of whom is a sorceress) and men who work odd jobs of questionable provenance.

Unemployed and out of money, the grandson gets sucked into the world of illegal workers. He soon finds himself at what the show calls Kalifoo Ground, which is the real-life area where undocumented workers meet each morning to wait for farmers and construction bosses to choose them for labor-intensive work, much like what happens outside of the Cara Mineo center in Sicily. The plots all follow a similar theme, where Lorenzo, stripped of his civil rights as an undocumented worker, has to skirt the system and learns quickly that the only way to survive is to live outside the rules. It would be hysterical if it weren't based entirely on fact.

There have been other creative interpretations of the dismal life in Castel Volturno. Most notably *Là-bas: A Criminal Education*, a drama by Neapolitan director Guido Lombardi. The film is the dark version of *Connection House*, showing the real tragedy where the web series finds the comedic silver lining. *Là-bas* won a Future Lion award at the Venice Film Festival and a Flash Forward award at Busan in 2011.

Those who do try to shine light on the grave situation are really islands in a sea of indifference. Even documentaries that focus on the migrant crisis, such as *Fire at Sea*, which was nominated for a Best Documentary Feature Oscar in 2016, tend to attract those who already care about migrants rather than spreading the true stories to a wider audience.

Katja Meier is a Swiss writer who self-published a book in 2014 called *Across the Deep Blue Sea: Good Intentions and Hard Lessons in an Italian Refugee Home* about her time helping out at a refugee center in rural Tuscany, where she lives with her Italian companion and their two sons. Her experience ended with her losing her job for bucking the system and trying to make the refugee center into something more like what Sister

Rita runs at Casa Ruth, where women can find a way forward. Two of the Nigerian women in the center were clearly in touch with pimps and madams. They received troubling calls and ran away, came back again, and then ran away once more. The others were constantly coming back to the shelter from weekends in the city with wads of cash that Katja had good reason to suspect was earned through prostitution.

I met with Katja after her book came out and we discussed the question of whether regulating sex work in Italy would help some of the women who are trafficked and protect those who chose sex work out of an absence of alternatives. I had never agreed with that theory, but she made me consider the fact that even though these women are not prostitutes in the true sense of the word, they quite possibly would be more protected if the industry was not just legal, but regulated. But she also recognizes the potential minefield of addressing sex worker rights in the context of sex-trafficked women.

Katja is convinced that the women she dealt with resorted to prostitution out of a sense of financial desperation. She says that, like many young girls who go to Los Angeles or London, the Nigerian girls she worked with seem to have come to Europe with what she describes as "dreams and goals like all young women their age." And if sex work was how they might achieve it, "that's what they would have to do."

If that's the case, that they weren't in fact trafficked but instead found themselves choosing sex work because it was the only way to financial stability, they would benefit from regularized prostitution and sex-worker benefits. The trouble is, it is almost impossible to know how many women choose prostitution, how many resort to prostitution when they have no money, and how many are truly trafficked.

The United Nations has done what it can to lay out precise boundaries when it comes to distinguishing between sex workers and those who are trafficked for sex. The UN "Protocol to Prevent, Suppress and Punish Trafficking in Persons", also referred to as one of a trio of Palermo protocols signed in 2000, defines human trafficking as "involving actions by a third party (e.g. recruitment, transportation); use of force, deception or other fraudulent means; and purposes of exploitation (e.g. forced labor)."

Writing on the topic in *The Lancet*, Shira M. Goldenberg, PhD, a gender specialist at Simon Fraser University and part of the Gender & Sexual Health Initiative of the British Columbia Centre for Excellence in HIV/AIDS, makes an important distinction. "The conflation of sex trafficking and sex work on an ideological and political basis has historically fueled repressive policies that have undermined efforts to advance the health and human rights of sex workers," she says.[78] Essentially, treating sex workers like women who have been trafficked denies legitimate workers important rights like safe work environments and the ability to pay into a structured health care system.

When I reached out to her for this book, she explained that most countries that have signed onto the Palermo Protocol should already have had existing laws in place to address trafficking in persons, which, she says, "certainly represents an egregious human rights violation and is known to occur among both men and women and across many different sectors of work." She says laws surrounding sex work should focus on legitimate prostitution, which she defines as the consensual exchange of sexual services between adults. "Conflation with trafficking and the singling out of the sex industry within dominant anti-trafficking discourse is often based on moral assumptions and political agendas, rather than evidence," she told me. "Rather than conflating sex work and trafficking, efforts to ensure access to safe working conditions and decriminalizing sex work can reduce marginalized individuals' potential vulnerability to workplace exploitation since they no longer have to operate in a clandestine fashion and have been widely demonstrated to promote the health and human rights of sex workers."

When women are identified as truly trafficked, the next

hurdle is what to do with them on a long-term basis. No one can live at Casa Ruth forever and other entities under the Church lean towards repatriating Nigerian women, which is a topic of considerable debate. Sister Eugenia Bonetti is an elderly Italian Consolata Missionary nun who spent a quarter of a century working in the slums in Kenya before being called back to Italy to work with the increasing number of Eastern European and other women working on the streets as prostitutes in central Italy. In 2000, she was asked to start a program called Slaves No More, to help rescue sex trafficking victims off the streets and get them out of detention centers. Now her group has an extensive network of nuns who work all over the world to help victims of trafficking.

In Rome, she and her nuns work tirelessly to free women from the notorious Ponte Galeria detention center on the outskirts of the city who are kept behind the type of reinforcement one might expect to see at a maximum-security facility for Mafia murderers. Most of the people who end up in Ponte Galeria have been convicted of crimes like petty theft and carrying false documents. They have invariably exhausted their opportunities within other migrant reception centers. If they end up in Ponte Galeria, they are at the end of the line. They will either be deported back to their countries of origin (if those countries accept them), or commit suicide waiting.

Sister Bonetti and her network of nuns have been counseling women here for more than a decade. When they can, they accompany the women who are being deported back to Nigeria where they are met by others in Sister Bonetti's group to offer them shelter while they try to plan their next steps. Going home is not easy for the women. Most often they try to get back to Europe.

Sending trafficked women back to Nigeria has drawbacks beyond the original lack of opportunity that led them into their trafficker's trap. First, if trafficked women are owned by a madam or took a JuJu curse, they could be killed for failing to fulfill their promises. I once met a woman waiting to be returned to Nigeria in the Ponte Galeria detention center who had received regular photos of a man holding a machete to her mother's neck demanding she repay her debts or her mother would die. Another woman waiting for deportation had decorated her holding cell with Christian verses and prayers. She wore multiple rosaries around her neck, clinging on to any hope at salvation from the JuJu curse that she could find. She was terrified that she would be killed when she returned. She had left the package required by most witch doctors of her personal bits, a few toenails and locks of pubic hair. She was sure that when the man who administered the curse saw her, he would take her life.

If their families knew they were forced into sex slavery, they could be rejected. Either way, going back is seen as a failure by most of the women, no matter how horrific their time in Europe may have been. The vast majority of the women who make it all the way to Italy only to be sent back are devastated.

Sister Rita also works closely with Sister Bonetti and is part of the Slaves No More network. When Blessing returned back to Nigeria with Pozzi the journalist, Slaves No More chronicled her journey as part of a campaign to show trafficked women that they can, indeed, go home. What they left out was the fact that Blessing, like so many other women, couldn't actually tell her parents what she'd been through. And while she spoke at a church similar to the one where her original recruiter found her, she sadly had little impact. As we've seen, even her own sister was almost trafficked in spite of knowing what can happen.

Sister Rita prefers to integrate women saved from the streets into Italian society, but she has sent a number of girls to Sister Bonetti who wish to return to Nigeria. IOM also repatriates people from Libya back to Nigeria. They only help those who volunteer to go back, meaning if the women are still en route to Europe, they don't stop them. But when they do send those who want to go back, they try to facilitate a smooth return when they can.

Slaves No More also works with the Italian group Talitha Kum, which, when translated from Aramaic, means "Little girl, I say to you, arise!" the words Jesus speaks to a twelve-year old paralytic in the Gospel of Mark before she gets up and walks, according to the Bible. The group has more than a thousand nuns and religious women active in seventy-one countries who provide shelter and counseling to help victims get out of sexual exploitation and try to carve out a new life. The group's leader, Sister Gabriella Bottani, has been especially focused on helping women to understand that they are victims and not to feel guilty for what they have done, no matter what their legal circumstances might be. "So often they don't even know they are victims," she says. "Some are in denial out of fear or anger or embarrassment, but getting them to admit they are being victimized is the first step in rescuing them."

Groups supported by the Catholic Church have been by far the most successful in helping to free women from sex trafficking. Catholic group Be Free Cooperative as well as the JPIC (Justice, Peace and Integrity of Creation) offer counseling for trafficked and abused women, and they have beds for those who need shelter. While there are groups to help rescue and shelter women, there are simply not enough to deal with the tens of thousands of trafficked women in Italy, and adequate prevention remains the biggest challenge and the only real way to stop the trafficking cycle.

In May 2017, Laura Boldrini, the speaker of the Chamber of Deputies in the Italian Parliament, visited Benin City and a village in Edo State on what was the first-ever goodwill trip by an Italian politician dedicated to stop trafficking.

I first met Boldrini on a cliff over a migrant shipwreck in Lampedusa when she was the Italian spokesperson for UNHCR. During the height of the Arab Spring arrivals, she was a constant point of reference. She could spout out statistics, phone numbers and perfect sound bites at the drop of a hat. She has not had an easy transition into politics, however, and is the frequent object of vitriol, both online and in person. Some of the abuse is because of her open-arms approach to migration, which does not sit well with a number of Italian lawmakers who tend more towards the right in their views. Other abuse is rooted in the sexism that is a standard feature in Italian society.

Fulvio Rustico, Italy's ambassador to Nigeria, who has been beating his head against a wall for years as he tries to work with his Nigerian counterparts, arranged Boldrini's trip. They met Julie Okah-Donli, the new director of Nigeria's National Agency for the Prohibition of Trafficking in Persons, known as NAPTIP.[79] The organization works on a limited national budget. In recent years, they have moved from awareness campaigns that often fell on deaf ears to active participation in the search for, and legal prosecution of, traffickers. In March 2017, they were instrumental in assuring the conviction of Serah Ekundayo Ezekiel, a woman who was found guilty of recruiting women to be trafficked to Italy. She was sentenced to seven years in prison, which is a success in and of itself, though her conviction remains one of very few success stories in Nigeria's efforts to stop trafficking.

Okah-Donli was tapped to lead the group in 2017 in an effort to revamp the entire anti-trafficking organization, which has itself been accused of employing complicit officers who are actually part of the trafficking rings. "We must collectively eradicate all forms of corruption within the system, especially in investigation of reported cases of trafficking," she said at her inaugural press conference in April 2017. "Any staff caught in this practice will be dealt with in line with the provisions of the civil service rule and thereafter handed over for further necessary action if found guilty."

The very fact that she felt obligated to address such corruption at the heart of the agency meant to stop trafficking underscores one of the greatest challenges. Coupled with corruption in Italy's own approach to the trafficking scheme, the women really stand no chance once they are on their way to Europe.

Okah-Donli has also insisted that Italy and other European nations who want to stop the flow of Nigerians to Europe must invest in Nigeria to create real jobs to give people a reason to stay. Despite being one of the richest African nations, they haven't been able to institute programs to create employment outside of the oil fields, which are controlled by the wealthy few.

Boldrini agrees to a certain extent, but her hands are tied. Italy's focus tends to echo Europe's sentiments that it is better to institute border controls first and then worry about making life behind the fences better. Countless attempts to invest in infrastructure in Libya to try to lend stability to that nation have proved fruitless as well. Italy, coming out of its own triple-dip recession, doesn't have a lot of spare cash to be generous with, especially in dealing with a bureaucracy that is even more corrupt than its own. Still, investing in Nigeria would almost certainly impact the trafficking flows.

If Okah-Donli's intentions bear fruit, it will be a major improvement for anti-trafficking efforts from within Nigeria. Under the old guard, NAPTIP processed just 4,755 trafficking investigations since the agency was created in 2003. Most of these are launched only after the women are repatriated back to Nigeria, either from Libya or Italy. Okah-Donli's new agenda addresses one of the major obstacles – warning young women in Nigeria that they are prime targets.

"As part of my vision concerning awareness creation, NAPTIP officers will commence a weekly sensitization campaign at diverse public places around the country," she promised. "In addition, the agency will launch a massive nation-wide campaign against human trafficking. NAPTIP will seek out Nigerians in market squares, town halls, village squares, schools, motor parks, churches, and so on."

"We will show pictures, engage them in local languages with

victims' stories. I will revamp our hotlines so that they can function like the ones you have in developed countries. Anytime any Nigerian calls, NAPTIP will not only answer, NAPTIP will respond."

Her promises, however noble, beg one question: what has the agency been doing until now?

NAPTIP says it works to "empower" these women upon their return, though most of the women would disagree. The UN's trafficking report also finds that many Nigerian women and children are taken to other western and central African countries, as well as to South Africa. There they are also trafficked for the commercial sex industry or for domestic servitude. The challenges are clearly enormous on both sides of the Sahara Desert.

During Boldrini's meeting, Okah-Donli admitted that they have not made enough progress in breaking the trafficking ring. The very fact that Facebook pages and other online forums exist that help facilitate the sale of these women through pictures and descriptions is appalling, but it also shows how sophisticated the trafficking network is and how it is able to operate with relative ease. "There must definitely be a cartel there. We have not been able to break through this cartel," she said. "We are looking for ways where we will partner more with these other countries where these girls are brought back from, so that we can break into this cartel and investigate deeper."[80] Again, the fact that this isn't already being done underscores the problem. Nigeria blames the Libyan smugglers who ferry the girls to Italy; in turn, Italy blames the traffickers in Nigeria.

The reality is that the only way to stop this horrific cycle is to stop trafficking at its roots. Trying to intercept it along the many trafficking routes is like trying to divert a river with tiny pebbles – the water will only find another way to flow. Italian judge Maria Grazia Giammarinaro served as the Special Representative and Coordinator for Combating Trafficking in Human Beings of the OSCE (Organization for Security and

Cooperation in Europe) from 2010 to 2014. Her findings were among the most profound and most often ignored observations about why trafficking exists. Speaking to a group of mostly women interested in trafficking at the end of her mandate, she pointed out what she thought must be done.

> I have reiterated what grass roots organizations and agencies operating within conflict-affected areas ... have been denouncing during the past few years, since the mass migration crisis erupted in Europe: trafficking in persons in conflict and crisis situations is not a mere possibility, but a consequence of crisis and conflict on a regular basis, which means that trafficking is a systemic outcome of conflict.[81]

One of the potential missed opportunities to intervene is surely on the NGO rescue boats. Doctors Without Borders does have an anti-trafficking specialist, Sarah Adeyinka, who frequently spends time on board their ships, but most of the NGO rescue ships do not have such experts. Adeyinka came into the job because her own cousin was trafficked from Nigeria to Libya. She ended up being repatriated back to Nigeria after a rare revolt against the trafficker in Libya, but Adeyinka, who was working with victims of sexual abuse before concentrating on trafficked women, has heard hundreds of stories from those onboard the ships who weren't so lucky. NGO workers say the obstacle in identifying trafficked women at the moment they are plucked from the sea is that the rescues are so dangerous and chaotic and the women are often injured or so traumatized that, even if they are obviously being trafficked, they may not accept that sort of truth at the time. One rescuer told me that she hated to be the one to tell them what might be happening because, first, she might be wrong, and second, because the rescue from the smuggler's ship is the only moment of relief most people feel on the whole journey. To be pulled from the water and then told they will most likely become a sex slave seems just too cruel. But I have to wonder if that's not an opportunity for action. If Joy, whom I met outside Cara Minea, had known on the rescue ship why she shouldn't call the number sewn into her jacket, she might have been saved sooner. To have dedicated people on every single rescue ship who are trained to intervene might only be a drop in the ocean, but at least it wouldn't leave all the heavy lifting to the nuns once the girls have already been exploited.

When I sat with IOM's Carlotta Santarossa and heard about the brochures they hand out when people are offloaded at Italian ports, I couldn't help but wonder why that sort of information isn't being given out on the rescue ships as well. The answer is simple: it's not the rescuer's mandate to identify trafficked women, it's to save people's lives. It's hard to argue with that point, and given that the NGOs only account for around a third of all rescues at sea, it's clear that the problem is immense. The other two-thirds of the migrants and refugees are picked up by the Italian Coast Guard, the EU's Frontex boats and passing merchant ships, none of which are in any sort of position to do much but get these people out of immediate danger.

Other anti-trafficking NGOs like Progetto Integrazione Accoglienza Migranti (PIAM), run by Princess and her husband, do try to meet women when they arrive in Italian ports, but it is next to impossible to know what the demographic make-up will be of those on the rescue ships or even where migrants will dock until the last minute because the Coast Guard's command center is often juggling multiple ships at the same time. It is also difficult to gain access to the reception areas, which tend to be in the military sections of the Italian ports.

Here, too, intervention at this stage of arrival rarely takes place, even though it could make a vital difference. The authorities who process the migrants at the port just don't have the manpower or the expertise to do more than move thousands of people through the process from rescue to asylum application.

Instead, the simple fact is that no one tells the girls they have likely been trafficked, even though everyone along the chain suspects they are. No one warns them that the phone number they are carrying will lead them to a madam pimp, debt bondage and sex slavery. No one takes them aside and asks questions.

And worse, even if a woman, at that moment, realizes she has been trafficked for sex, she has so few options. She cannot go back across the sea, back through Libya and the desert towards home. No migrant caravans head in the opposite direction. At this point, she must still go forward through the legal asylum process and hope for the best, trying not to fall into a trap that catches almost everyone.

CAST OF CHARACTERS

NIGERIAN SEX TRAFFICKING VICTIMS (NAMES HAVE BEEN CHANGED IN SOME CASES)

Dolly – arrived by smuggler ship to Lampedusa in 2011 and went on to become a window girl in Amsterdam before leaving prostitution to get married.

Joy – rescued by Italian coastguards from a sinking rubber raft and placed at CARA Mineo Center for Asylum Seekers from where she was identified as a victim of trafficking in an Italian police operation called Skin Trade in 2016 and later gave testimony against her traffickers.

Betsy – trafficked at the age of fourteen and rescued from the Domitiana when she was six months pregnant, gave birth to a daughter called Faith.

Rose – escaped from the Domitiana with her boyfriend after being beaten by her madam, was later abused again by a corrupt cleaning company while working at an American military unit based near Naples.

Favour – came to Italy by way of Lampedusa and was found strangled and burned in Parco della Favorita in Palermo. Her body was later stolen from a city morgue.

Holly – testified about arms trafficking in and around Castel Volturno after being forced to perform sex acts on a bed over a cache of grenades and arms.

Loveth – fifteen-year-old murdered in Palermo in likely revenge killing after her trafficked mother tried to leave her madam.

Beauty – mother of Emanuele, saved from the Domitiana by Sister Rita.

Honey – saved from the Domitiana by Sister Rita, became a cook at Casa Ruth.

Blessing Okoedion – advocate for victims' rights and author of *The Courage of Freedom* about her escape from sex traffickers on the Domitiana.

Princess Inyang Okonon – advocate for victims' rights and co-founder of PIAM Onlus, which helps rescue sex trafficked women in northern Italy.

MAMANS, MADAMS AND OTHER SEX TRAFFICKERS

Most victims of sex trafficking never know their madams' real names. These names represent those who appear in court documents, interviews and the victims' recollections.

Maman Alice – recruiter in Nigeria who arranged for Blessing's false visa and transportation to Spain and Italy.

Maman Glory – recruiter in Spain who helped facilitate Blessing's transfer to Italy.

Mamma Lucky – former madam who ran a shop on the Domitiana selling ethnic food and objects used in the JuJu curse. She died in 2016 and is buried in a section for unnamed migrants in Pozzuoli cemetery.

Madam Faith – the Nigerian madam who owned Blessing in Castel Volturno.

Madam Pamela – real name Gift Akoro, a twenty-eight-year-old madam who was arrested under operation Skin Trade. She had a list of the names of young women expected to arrive by migrant vessel in her possession when she was arrested.

Madam Juliet – real name Toyin Lokiki, a thirty-one-year-old madam who was arrested under operation Skin Trade. She had JuJu curse relics in her possession.

Lady Ga Ga – a madam who operated out of a hair salon next to the Ob Ob Fashion Tailor Shop on the Domitiana in 2008 when Camorra gunmen massacred six African men.

Serah Ekundayo Ezekiel – one of the very few women convicted by Nigeria's National Agency for the Prohibition of Trafficking in Persons (NAPTIP) for recruiting and trafficking women to Italy. She was sentenced to seven years in prison.

THE NUNS

Sister Rita Giaretta – Catholic nun and member of the Ursuline Sister order who co-founded and runs Casa Ruth in Caserta.

Sister Assunta – Catholic nun and member of Ursuline Sister order who assists women at Casa Ruth in Caserta.

Sister Eugenia Bonetti – Catholic nun and member of the Consolata Missionary Sister order who founded the anti-trafficking organization Slaves No More.

THE MAFIA

Camorra – Italian organized crime syndicate that operates around Naples.

Cosa Nostra – Italian Mafia organization that operates in Sicily.

'Ndrangheta – Italian organized crime syndicate that operates in Calabria.

Sacra Corona – Italian organized crime syndicate that operated in Puglia until the early 2000s, now replaced by a myriad of criminal gangs.

Mafia Capitale – criminal organization operating in Rome.

Salvatore Buzzi – head of Mafia Capitale, convicted of siphoning off funds intended for migrant and refugee support.

Vittorio Casamonica – Roman mobster buried in an extravagant funeral in Rome in 2015.

Alfonso Cesarano – Camorra gunman convicted of killing six African men at the Ob Ob Exotic Fashion Tailor Shop in September 2008. Serving life sentence in prison.

Francesco Chianese – fruit vendor and Camorra associate thought to have trained militias in Libya and Nigeria, well known to Nigerian gangs in Castel Volturno, linked to Jihadist cell in France. Smuggled arms to Naples in extra-large Nigerian potatoes. Arrested in May 2016.

Pupetta Maresca – known as Lady Camorra, murdered her Mafia husband's killer. Lives in Sorrento on the Amalfi Coast.

Bernardo Provenzano – boss of Sicilian Mafia arrested in 2006 after forty-three years on the run from law enforcement.

THE NIGERIAN GANGS

Black Axe – known for wearing black and red ribbons, first to arrive in Italy, originated from rebellious gangs in university communities in Nigeria, focused on sex and drugs trafficking.

EIYE – known for wearing black hats.

Maphite – known for wearing red and green, based in northern Italy near Turin.

Black Cats – Nigerian gang that handles large orders of illicit drugs brought in from West Africa. Assists in smuggling of trafficked women. Local Italian boss thought to be a madam in Castel Volturno.

Ameyaw Bismark (Kelly) – former leader of Black Axe gang working with Camorra in sex and drugs trafficking; in Italian prison.

Bongo Issaka – former second in command of Black Axe gang working with Camorra; in Italian prison.

Kennedy Osazi – trafficker with the EIYE gang in Castel Volturno recruiting Nigerian men to push heroin and purchase trafficked women; in Italian prison.

Collins Twumasi – Nigerian member of EIYE gang who turned himself in and gave evidence about how he and others buy and sell trafficked women. Serving ten-year sentence in Italian prison system.

ALLEGED ARMS AND DRUGS TRAFFICKERS

Mario di Leva and Anna Maria Fontana – also known as Jafaar and the Veiled Lady or Dark Lady. Italian couple who converted to Islam and were radicalized in Libya. Di Leva was a former Freemason and Fontana was a council woman. Arrested in February 2017 for trafficking arms, modified helicopters and large-scale munitions to foreign fighters throughout Europe and to militias in Libya and Iran.

Luca di Leva – son of Mario di Leva and Anna Maria Fontana, arrested in connection with family's arms trafficking business.

Andrea Pardi – owner of Italiana Elicotteri helicopter dealership and tied to Mario di Leva and Anna Maria Fontana's arms trafficking business. Arrested in February 2017.

Ali Mohamud Shaswish – Libyan middleman tied to arms trafficking business with Andrea Pardi, Mario di Leva and Anna Maria Fontana. Whereabouts unknown.

Abu Walid – human smuggler in Tripoli who refused to take foreign fighters to Italy because of the low pay offered by an ISIS agent. Whereabouts unknown.

ALLEGED AND CONVICTED TERRORISTS

Anas El Abboubi – jihadi rapper and recruiter known to Italian anti-terrorist investigators; attended Islamic Cultural Center in

Brescia and launched Sharia4Italia recruitment website. Disappeared after going to Syria in 2015.

Salah Abdeslam – Belgium-born French national of Moroccan descent, connected to the 2015 Paris attacks and arrested in Brussels in 2016. He traveled to Bari, Italy, by ferry from Greece in 2015. In a Belgian prison.

Amponsah – code name for the man producing false documents out of a hidden factory near Naples that he sells on the deep Web. Whereabouts unknown.

Anis Amri – Tunisian-born terrorist who came to Italy via Lampedusa in 2011. Radicalized in a Palermo prison and killed twelve people by ramming a stolen truck into a Christmas market in Berlin. Killed by Italian police in Milan in December 2016.

'Jo' – pseudonym for Liberian child soldier who testified to Italian police about the illicit arms trade in and around Castel Volturno.

Mohamed Lahlaoui – Moroccan man arrested in March 2016 on terrorism charges in Germany after being given a deportation notice from Brescia, Italy, in 2014 related to weapons and drug trafficking charges. Attended Islamic Cultural center in Brescia. In German prison.

Khalid El Bakraoui – Belgian national of Moroccan descent, suicide bomber at Brussels subway attack in March 2016. His last call before detonating himself was to Mohamed Lahlaoui; expelled from Italy in 2014.

Saber Hmidi – Tunisian inmate in Italian jail system suspected of recruiting and radicalizing young inmates. In isolation in unnamed maximum security Italian prison.

Djamal Eddine Ouali – Algerian illegally residing in Italy, arrested in Salerno in March 2016 on suspicion of supplying false documents to Brussels airport suicide bombers. Extradited to Belgium in 2016.

Youssef Zaghba – Italian-Moroccan terrorist responsible for June 2017 attack on London Bridge that killed eight people. Was a patron of Sharia4Italia website and Jihadi rapper Abboubi's music. Killed by police the night of the attack.

KEY STATE PLAYERS

Laura Boldrini – former spokesperson for UNHCR (the UN Refugee Agency) in Lampedusa. President of Italy's Chamber of Deputies, traveled to Nigeria in 2017 to initiate efforts to combat sex trafficking.

Maria Grazia Giammarinaro – Special Representative and Coordinator for Combating Trafficking in Human Beings with the Organization for Security and Cooperation in Europe (OSCE).

Guido Longo – police commissioner in Palermo working to unravel ties between Sicilian Mafia and Nigerian gangs.

Sebastiano Maccarrone – Director of CARA Mineo Reception Center for Asylum Seekers accused of mishandling funds intended for refugees.

Catello Maresca – Head of the Naples anti-Mafia and anti-terrorism unit.

Franco Roberti – prominent state prosecutor and head of Italy's Direzione Nazionale Antimafia (national anti-Mafia organization).

Carmelo Zuccaro – chief investigating prosecutor of Catania, Sicily; believes rescue ships should not actively search for migrants, launched first formal investigation into NGO activities at sea.

KEY LOCATIONS NEAR NAPLES AND IN SICILY

Mezzogiorno – the southern regions of Italy encompassing Abruzzo, Basilicata, Calabria, Campania, Molise, Puglia and Sicily.

Land of Fires – the largest illegal waste dump in Europe, encompassing an area between Mt Vesuvius and Caserta where more than 550,000 people live; also encompasses the Camorra's key territory.

Domitiana – a twenty-mile stretch of road extending north from Castel Volturno towards Rome and south to Naples, laid over an ancient Roman roadway built by the Emperor Domitian in AD95 that meets the ancient Appian Way south of Rome.

Castel Volturno – city dissected by the Domitiana in Campania along the coast near Naples.

Coppola Village (also known as Pinetamare) – failed utopian village in Castel Volturno built illegally by Vincenzo and Cristoforo Coppola in the 1960s.

Ob Ob Exotic Fashions Tailor Shop – men's tailor shop on the Via Domitiana where six African immigrants were shot in 2008 by the Camorra.

Caserta – city in Campania thirty kilometers from Castel Volturno, thirty-five kilometers from Naples.

Lampedusa – the largest of Italy's Pelagie Islands belonging to the region of Sicily. In the 2000s, the island became the primary entry point into Europe for migrants and refugees leaving the North African coast.

TO HELP

Please consider making a donation to these groups that work to help victims of sex trafficking in Italy.

ORGANIZATIONS IN ITALY WORKING WITH SEX-TRAFFICKED WOMEN

Be Aware now
www.beawarenow.eu
Be Aware Now strives to raise awareness of public issues and to promote human rights, in Italy and around the world.

Casa Ruth
www.associazionerut.it
Welcome center and shelter for migrant women alone or with children who are victims of trafficking.

New Hope Cooperative
www.coop-newhope.it
Cooperative sponsored by Casa Ruth with a tailor shop that creates ethnic fashions by migrants and women who are victims of sex trafficking.

Mondo Senza Confini – Centro Miriam Makeba
World cultural center along the Via Domitiana in Castel Volturno dedicated to the memory of Miriam Makeba where

cultural events aimed at greater integration and understanding are held.

Slaves No More
www.slavesnomore.it
Catholic association against sexual violence and exploitation and trafficking of women aimed at prevention and integration of victims in society.

Be Free Cooperative Rome
www.befreecooperativa.org
Social cooperative sponsored by the Catholic Church focused on stopping violence against women, sex trafficking and discrimination.

Talitha Kum
www.talithakum.info
Global network of those in consecrated life in the Catholic Church working against trafficking of humans.

Centro Fernandes in Castel Volturno
www.centrofernandes.it
Migrant center sponsored by the Catholic diocese of Capua focused on education, integration, health and legal concerns of the area's vast documented and undocumented immigrant population. Sponsors Speranza or Hope project for women rescued from the Domitiana.

PIAM
www.piamonlus.org
Organization based in Asti in northern Italy rescuing and assisting sex trafficked women.

Community of Sant Egidio
www.santegidio.org

Organization established in 1968 dedicated to the poor and migrant and refugee communities with a special focus on victims of trafficking; working directly with the Vatican.

Jerry Essan Masslo Association
www.associazionejerrymasslo.it
Organization named after a South African migrant, who was murdered in 1989 near Caserta in racist violence at the hands of the Camorra, facilitating integration between African and Italian communities in southern Italy.

INTERNATIONAL ORGANIZATIONS DIRECTLY ASSISTING MIGRANTS, REFUGEES AND VICTIMS OF TRAFFICKING

OSCE – Organization for Security and Cooperation in Europe

UNHCR – United Nations High Commissioner for Refugees

UNICEF – United Nations International Children's Emergency Fund

UNODC – United Nations Office on Drugs and Crime

IOM – International Organization for Migration (also called the U.N. Migration agency).

Save the Children – UK-based organization working with unaccompanied minors within the migrant community.

Mobile Offshore Aid Station (MOAS) – Malta-based organization founded in 2014 by an American-Italian couple for the purpose of search and rescue.

S.O.S. Méditerranée – Gibraltar-based French humanitarian organization launched in 2015 with one rescue ship working in collaboration with Doctors Without Borders.

Doctors Without Borders or Médecins Sans Frontières (MSF) – international humanitarian organization supplying medical professionals to war-torn areas, launched Mediterranean sea rescue operations in 2015.

Lifeboat Project – German international maritime rescue operation working in the Mediterranean under the International Maritime Rescue Mixed Migrant Safety Project.

Sea Eye – based in the Netherlands, started search and rescue operations in 2016.

Proactiva Open Arms – based in Spain, part of the Human Rights At Sea initiative, launched search and rescue operations in 2016.

Sea Watch – founded by three private business partners in Germany in 2015 to take part in search and rescue operations off the coast of Libya.

ACKNOWLEDGMENTS

The official definition of a refugee is someone forced to flee conflict or persecution who cannot safely return back home. The definition of a migrant is someone who chooses to move to improve his or her life. I have interviewed countless victims of sex trafficking who may fall into either category, but who fit neither description, and I thank each and every one of them who told me their painful stories, whether they appear in this book or not.

There are many people I cannot thank by name for their immense help, including the victims both saved and still captive whose names are changed here to protect them from revenge and/or deportation. I also thank, but cannot name, the undercover police officers who kept me safe in Castel Volturno, Caserta and Palermo, for being my guides through a world I could not have traversed alone.

I thank everyone who is quoted in the book for their time, but especially Sister Rita and Sister Assunta at Casa Ruth in Caserta, who opened their home and their hearts to me and restored my faith in many things. They deserve an outpouring of respect (and donations) for all they do with virtually no help from anyone. Without their shelter and dedication, I shudder to think how many women, and especially their babies, wouldn't survive.

A very special thank you to Blessing Okoedion, whose strength and determination (and occasional lectures) guided and inspired me and kept me focused on the human side of this tragedy. She could have walked away when she was rescued. Instead, she continues to make a difference in the lives of so many other victims.

Andrea Pastorelli was instrumental in keeping me on the right side of the line that separates sex trafficking and sex work. It is because of his crucial advice and experience with sex worker rights for the United Nations Development Programme (UNDP) throughout China and in New York that I do not refer to the victims of sex trafficking as prostitutes.

I also thank those aid workers who helped me along the way, especially Mathilde Auvillain of S.O.S. Mediterranée, Flavio di Giacomo of IOM and cultural mediator Sarah Adeyinka. I also thank Father Thomas Rosica, whose perspective proved an important aspect in the telling of this story.

Turning my notebooks full of interviews and stories into a coherent book would not have been possible without Rayhané Sanders at Massie & McQuilkin, an inspiring agent who wouldn't let me give up. I am also indebted to Shadi Doostdar at Oneworld who so expertly whipped this manuscript into shape with the critical eye of a journalist and the expertise of a publisher. I am grateful to my editors at The Daily Beast, CNN and *Scientific American* who have supported this project and continue to let me tell stories about the migrant crisis in Italy.

Thank you to my sister Sherri Stekl, my most trusted advisor, who graciously read this manuscript at various stages to give me the honest truth about what worked and what didn't.

Not least, I owe a world of gratitude to my teenage sons who sacrificed the time I should have spent with them so I could research and write this book. Nicholas, seventeen, was able to help me draw up the outline for this book and Matthew, fifteen, was a daily reminder of the exciting journey through adolescence on which many of the girls forced into sexual slavery so poignantly miss out.

NOTES

1 UNHCR, "Operational Portal Refugee Situations," 2017 http://data2.unhcr.org/en/situations/mediterranean/location/5205 [accessed 4 August 2017]

2 The Borgen Project, "Poverty in Italy," 2014 https://www.borgenproject.org/poverty-italy [accessed 4 August 2017]

3 B. Boucher, "Italian Mafia Helps Arm ISIS With Looted Antiquities," ArtNet News, 2016 https://www.news.artnet.com/market/italian-mafia-arms-isis-trading-art-707582 [accessed 4 August 2017]

4 B. Nadeau, "Italy's New Immigration Crisis," *Newsweek*, 2009 http://www.newsweek.com/italys-new-immigration-crisis-78305 [accessed 4 August 2017]

5 Amnesty International, "Central Mediterranean: Death Toll Soars as EU Turns its Back on Refugees and Migrants," 2017 http://www.amnesty.eu/en/news/press-releases/eu/asylum-and-migration/central-mediterranean-death-toll-soars-as-eu-turns-its-back-on-refugees-and-migrants-1056/#.WXsgTFHTWUk [accessed 5 May 2017]

6 Global Economic Prospects, World Bank Group, "Gross Domestic Product 2016," World Bank, 2016 http://databank.worldbank.org/data/download/GDP.pdf [accessed 17 April 2017]

7 US Department of State, "Trafficking in Persons 2014 Report: Country Narratives Nigeria," 2014 https://www.state.gov/j/tip/rls/tiprpt/countries/2014/226790.htm [accessed 4 August 2017]

8 Author interview at Cara di Mineo, Sicily, December 2015

9 Central Intelligence Agency, "World Factbook: Nigeria," 2014 https://www.cia.gov/library/publications/the-world-factbook/fields/2122.html [accessed 25 July 2017]

10 "Marinai Residence – Sigonella Housing Information Page," Facebook, 2013 https://www.facebook.com/sigonella.marinai2001/ [accessed 4 August 2017]

11 A. Mazzeo, "Grandi Affari a Mineo Con Il Villaggio Dei Marines Di Sigonella," I Padrini del Ponte, 2010 http://www.antoniomazzeoblog.blogspot.it/2010/10/grandi-affari-mineo-con-il-villaggio.html [accessed 20 May 2016]

12 R. Ferdman, "Spain's Black Market Economy Is Worth 20% of its GDP," *The Atlantic*, 2013 https://www.theatlantic.com/business/archive/2013/07/spains-black-market-economy-is-worth-20-of-its-gdp/277840/ [accessed 4 August 2017]

13 B. Natale, "Stupro Di Gruppo Al Cara Di Mineo: Arrestati Quattro Nigeriani," *La Repubblica* http://www.palermo.repubblica.it/cronaca/2016/12/17/news/stupro_di_gruppo_al_cara_di_mineo_arrestati_quattro_nigeriani-154306893 [accessed 17 December 2016]

14 European Commission: Migration and Home Affairs, "Country Responsible For Asylum Application (Dublin)," https://ec.europa.eu/home-affairs/what-we-do/policies/asylum/examination-of-applicants_en [accessed 2 March 2017]

15 "European Court of Justice Rules Against 'Humanitarian' Visas for Refugees," Deutsche Welle http://www.dw.com/en/european-court-of-justice-rules-against-humanitarian-visas-for-refugees/a-37834318 [accessed 7 March 2017]

16 European Commission: Migration and Home Affairs, "Identification of Applicants (EURODAC)," 2016 https://ec.europa.eu/home-affairs/what-we-do/policies/asylum/identification-of-applicants_en [accessed 4 August 2017]

17 H. Dijstelbloem, "Migration Tracking is a Mess," *Nature* http://www.nature.com/news/migration-tracking-is-a-mess-1.21542 [accessed 4 March 2017]

18 L. Sanders, "Anis Amri Habitually Took Drugs Before Berlin Attack, Say Italian Prosecutors," Deutsche Welle http://www.dw.com/en/anis-amri-habitually-took-drugs-before-berlin-attack-say-italian-prosecutors/a-37809997 [accessed 4 March 2017]

19 A. Lanni, "5 Things You Should Know About (Second-Class) Nigerian Migrants," Open Migration, 2015 http://openmigration.org/en/analyses/5-things-you-should-know-about-second-class-nigerian-migrants/ [accessed 4 August 2017]

20 France 24, "Hungary: Shocking Footage Shows Hungarian Police Throwing Bread at Desperate Refugees," YouTube, 2015 https://www.youtube.com/watch?v=kcRNfNS6HWo [accessed 4 August 2017]

21 G. Chiodini, et al., "Magmas Near the Critical Degassing Pressure Drive Volcanic Unrest Towards a Critical State," *Nature*, 2016 https://www.nature.com/articles/ncomms13712 [accessed 20 December 2016]

22 University of Chicago Press Journals, "Volcanoes wiped out Neanderthals, new study suggests," Science Daily, 2010 www.sciencedaily.com/releases/2010/10/101006094057.htm [accessed 4 August 2017]

23 G. Majori, "Short History of Malaria and its Eradication in Italy With Short Notes on the Fight Against the Infection in the Mediterranean Basin," US National Library of Medicine National Institutes of Health, 2012 https://www.ncbi.nlm.nih.gov/pmc/articles/PMC3340992/ [accessed 4 August 2017]

24 Carnegie Council for Ethics in International Affairs, "The Rockefeller Foundation in Sardinia: Pesticide Politics in the Struggle Against Malaria," 2005 https://www.carnegiecouncil.org/publications/articles_papers_reports/5117 [accessed 4 August 2017]

25 *Castel Volturno: Documentary Villaggio Coppola*, YouTube, 2013 https://www.youtube.com/watch?v=OU76H7mrijQ [accessed 4 August 2017]

26 V. Ammaliato, "Castelvolturno: Ecco il Quartiere Fantasma," Agora Vox, 2011 http://www.agoravox.it/Ecco-il-quartiere-fantasma.html [accessed 4 August 2017]

27 B. Nadeau, "The Mafia Plants Death in Italy's Land of Mozzarella," The Daily Beast, 2014 http://www.thedailybeast.com/articles/2014/03/20/the-mafia-plants-death-in-italy-s-land-of-mozzarella [accessed 4 August 2017]

28 A. Mossino, "Our History: In 1999 We Started Our Activity From the Emergency," PIAM Onlus http://www.piamonlus.org/news [accessed 4 August 2017]

29 http://www.piamonlus.org/ [accessed 4 August 2017]

30 "Operazione Skin Trade," Polizia Di Stato http://www.poliziadistato.it/articolo/1543581099f8a1d03597294820 [accessed 4 August 2017]

31 L. Distefano, "Riti Voodoo E Prostituzione Arrestati 11 'trafficanti di donne'," Live Sicilia http://www.catania.livesicilia.it/2016/10/24/riti-voodoo-e-prostituzione-arrestati-15-trafficanti-di-donne_393373 [accessed 4 August 2017]

32 S. Busari, "Woman Who Rescues 'Witch Children' Voted World's Most Inspirational Person," CNN http://edition.cnn.com/2016/02/16/africa/child-witchcraft-nigeria/ [accessed 4 August 2017]

33 C. Baarda, "Human trafficking for sexual exploitation from Nigeria into Western Europe: The role of voodoo rituals in the functioning of a criminal network," *European Journal of Criminology*, 2015 https://www.researchgate.net/publication/284419256_Human_trafficking_for_sexual_exploitation_from_Nigeria_into_Western_Europe_The_role_of_voodoo_rituals_in_the_functioning_of_a_criminal_network [accessed 4 August 2017]

34 TGCOM 24, "Napoli, Allarme Sette Sataniche: Fedeli Lanciano Esorcismo Dall'Elicottero," Mediaset http://www.tgcom24.mediaset.it/cronaca/campania/napoli-allarme-sette-sataniche-fedeli-lanciano-esorcismo-dall-elicottero_2123162-201502a.shtml [accessed 4 August 2017]

35 "Rite of Exorcism," Catholic Online http://www.catholic.org/prayers/prayer.php?p=683 [accessed 4 August 2017]

36 European Federation of Food, Agriculture and Tourism Trade Unions, "25 years after Jerry Masslo's death, FLAI CGIL Continues the Fight for Equal Treatment of Migrant Workers," 2014 http://www.effat.org/en/node/13636 [accessed 4 August 2017]

37 "Corruption Perceptions Index 2016," Transparency International https://www.transparency.org/news/feature/corruption_perceptions_index_2016 [accessed 4 August 2017]

38 J. Politi and V. Houlder, "Google Agrees €306m Italian Tax Settlement," *Financial Times* https://www.ft.com/content/4adb933e-30d0-11e7-9555-23ef563ecf9a [accessed 4 August 2017]

39 M. Ahmed and R. Sanderson, "Apple Agrees to Pay €318m Fine to Close Italian Tax Case," *Financial Times* https://www.ft.com/content/a38fa412-aef3-11e5-b955-1a1d298b6250 [accessed 4 August 2017]

40 F. Bruni, "The Filthy Metaphor of Rome," *New York Times* https://www.nytimes.com/2017/05/10/opinion/the-filthy-metaphor-of-rome.html [accessed 4 August 2017]

41 "Italy Busts 'Mafia Operation' in Large Migrant Center in Calabria," Deutsche Welle via Info Migrants http://www.infomigrants.net/en/post/3192/italy-busts-mafia-operation-in-large-migrant-center-in-calabria [accessed 4 August 2017]

42 "Child Killing Shows Mafia 'Code of Conduct' Is A Myth," AFP via The Local https://www.thelocal.it/20140320/child-killing-shows-mafia-code-of-conduct-is-myth [accessed 4 August 2017]

43 B. Nadeau, "Italian Police Probe Vatican, Mafia Links in Teen's Disappearance 30 Years Ago," The Daily Beast http://www.thedailybeast.com/italian-police-probe-vatican-mafia-links-in-teens-disappearance-30-years-ago [accessed 4 August 2017]

44 B. Nadeau, "Did Pope Francis Perform a Miracle in Naples?" CNN http://edition.cnn.com/videos/world/2015/03/22/lok-nadeau-pope-naples.cnn [accessed 4 August 2017]

45 U. Savona Ernesto and Riccardi Michele, "From Illegal Markets to Legitimate Businesses: The Portfolio of Organised Crime in Europe," Final Report of Project OCP, 2015 http://www.ocportfolio.eu [accessed 4 August 2017]

46 France 24, "Naples mafia may be behind killing of six Africans," http://www.france24.com/en/20080920-naples-mafia-may-be-behind-killing-six-africans-italy-mafia [accessed 4 August 2017]

47 "Rural Poverty in Naples," Rural Poverty Portal/I.F.A.D., 2014 http://www.ruralpovertyportal.org/web/rural-poverty-portal/country/home/tags/nigeria [accessed 4 August 2017]

48 (Judge) V. Alabiso, "Sezione del Giudice per le indagni preliminary Ufficio XIII ordinanze applicative di misura cautelare ordinanze applicative di misura cautelare," Tribunal of Naples

49 Nigeria's National Agency for the Prohibition of Trafficking in Persons (NAPTIP) http://www.naptip.gov.ng/ [accessed 4 August 2017]

50 "Human Trafficking in Numbers," Human Rights First, 2017 http://www.humanrightsfirst.org/resource/human-trafficking-numbers [accessed 4 August 2017]

51 *Worst Projects 2 – Real Ghetto – Castel Volturno Crack House*, YouTube https://www.youtube.com/watch?v=NSNHf3qbzj4 [accessed 4 August 2017]

52 A. De Simone, "A Castelvolturno il Supermarket Dell'Eroina Gestito Dalla Mafia Nigeriana," Corriere Della Sera TV http://video.corriere.it/a-castelvolturno-supermarket-dell-eroina-gestito-mafia-nigeriana/932bd8c4-c1aa-11e5-b5ee-f9f31615caf8 [accessed 4 August 2017]

53 "Transnational Organized Crime in West Africa: A Threat Assessment," United Nations Office on Drugs and Crime, 2013 https://www.unodc.org/documents/data-and-analysis/tocta/West_Africa_TOCTA_2013_EN.pdf [accessed 4 August 2017]

54 J. Cañas, "The Fight Against Spain's Increasingly Brazen Drug Traffickers," El Pais https://elpais.com/elpais/2017/04/26/inenglish/1493218501_067071.html [accessed 4 August 2017]

55 R. Callimachi and L. Tondo, "Scaling Up a Drug Trade, Straight Through ISIS Turf," New York Times https://www.nytimes.com/2016/09/14/world/europe/italy-morocco-isis-drug-trade.html [accessed 4 August 2017]

56 B. Nadeau, "Inside Europe's Heroin Capital," Newsweek http://www.newsweek.com/inside-europes-heroin-capital-82831 [accessed 4 August 2017]

57 A. De Simone, "Ecco Come Le Armi di ISIS e BOKO Haram Arrivano in Europa e in Italia," Corriere Della Sera TV http://video.corriere.it/ecco-come-le-armi-di-isis-e-boko-haram-arrivano-in-europa-e-in-italia/4ed42104-3041-11e5-8ebc-a14255a4c77f [accessed 4 August 2017]

58 B. Nadeau, "The Camorra-Connected Couple Running Guns – and Choppers – to ISIS," The Daily Beast http://www.thedailybeast.com/articles/2017/02/06/the-camorra-connected-couple-running-guns-and-choppers-to-isis.html [accessed 4 August 2017]

59 "Pan-Italy Raids Against 'Arms Trafficking Gang'," ANSA http://www.ansa.it/english/news/2015/11/12/pan-italy-raids-agst-arms-trafficking-gang-3_b3694df3-8111-4a7f-82bd-08b8e2f107c5.html [accessed 4 August 2017]

60 A. Smale, "Terrorism Suspects Are Posing as Refugees, Germany Says," New York Times http://www.nytimes.com/2016/02/06/world/europe/germany-refugees-isis.html?_r=0 [accessed 4 August 2017]

61 N. P. Walsh, "ISIS on Europe's Doorstep: How Terror is Infiltrating the Migrant Route," CNN http://edition.cnn.com/2016/05/26/middleeast/libya-isis-europe-doorstep/ [accessed 4 August 2017]

62 B. Nadeau, "ISIS. Can Buy UK Passports on the Deep Web to Thwart Brexit Security," The Daily Beast http://www.thedailybeast.com/articles/2017/02/10/isis-can-buy-u-k-passports-on-the-deep-web-to-thwart-brexit-security.html [accessed 4 August 2017]

63 "Corruption Perceptions Index 2016: Nigeria," Transparency International, https://www.transparency.org/country/NGA [accessed 4 August 2017]

64 "Organized Crime III: Confronting Organized Crime in Southern Italy," Public Library of US Diplomacy Cable via WikiLeaks https://wikileaks.org/plusd/cables/08NAPLES38_a.html [accessed 4 August 2017]

65 B. Nadeau, "Is Italy Enabling the ISIS Invasion of Europe?" The Daily Beast http://www.thedailybeast.com/is-italy-enabling-the-isis-invasion-of-europe [accessed 4 August 2017]

66 E. MacAskill, "ISIS. Document Leak Reportedly Reveals Identities of 22,000 Recruits," The Guardian https://www.theguardian.com/world/2016/mar/09/isis-document-leak-reportedly-reveals-identities-syria-22000-fighters [accessed 4 August 2017]

67 B. Nadeau, "London Terrorist Youssef Zaghba's Mom: 'How did it Come to This?'," The Daily Beast http://www.thedailybeast.com/london-terrorist-youssef-zaghbas-mom-how-did-it-come-to-this [accessed 4 August 2017]

68 B. Nadeau, "Berlusconi Sex Charges: The Bunga-Bunga Trial Begins," The Daily Beast http://www.thedailybeast.com/berlusconi-sex-charges-the-bunga-bunga-trial-begins [accessed 4 August 2017]

69 B. Nadeau, "Italy's Gruesome Migrant Organ Transplant Murders," The Daily Beast http://www.thedailybeast.com/articles/2016/07/06/italy-s-gruesome-migrant-organ-transplant-murders [accessed 4 August 2017]

70 "Nine Somalis Dumped in Egyptian Sea After Kidnapped and Organs Removed by Traffickers in Egypt," Ayyaantuu News http://ayyaantuu.net/nine-somalis-dumped-in-egyptian-sea-after-kidnapped-and-organs-removed-by-traffickers-in-egypt/ [accessed 4 August 2017]

71 S. Gandolfi, "I Clienti Delle Prostitute: chi sono, cosa cercano e perché (anche con minorenni)?" Corriere Della Sera http://27esimaora.corriere.it/articolo/i-clienti-delle-prostitute-chi-sono-cosa-cercano-e-perche-anche-con-minorenni/ [accessed 4 August 2017]

72 New Hope Cooperative http://www.coop-newhope.it/ [accessed 4 August 2017]

73 Emergency http://www.emergency.it/en-index.html [accessed 4 August 2017]

74 Mondo Senza Confini – Miriam Makeba Center https://www.facebook.com/Mondo-senza-confini-Centro-Miriam-Makeba-238752519525993/ [accessed 4 August 2017]

75 Fernandes Center http://www.centrofernandes.it/ [accessed 4 August 2017]

76 Miriam Makeba Visit ai Centro Fernandes, YouTube, https://www.youtube.com/watch?v=AQzvAC6UmrA [accessed 4 August 2017]

77 "Ecco 'Connection House', web-serie sugli immigrati di Castel Volturno," Il Mattino http://www.ilmattino.it/caserta/ecco_connection_house_la_web_serie_sugli_immigrati_di_castel_volturno-1918894.html [accessed 4 August 2017]

78 S. Goldenberg, "Trafficking, Migration and Health: Complexities and Future Directions," The Lancet Global Health, 3(3), 2015 http://www.thelancet.com/journals/langlo/article/PIIS2214-109X(15)70082-3/abstract [accessed 4 August 2017]

79 National Agency for the Prohibition of Trafficking in Persons http://www.naptip.gov.ng/ [accessed 4 August 2017]

80 "Italy to Support Nigeria in Fight Against Trafficking," Africa Independent Television   http://www.aitonline.tv/post-italy_to_support_nigeria_in_fight_against_trafficking [accessed 4 August 2017]

81 United Nations Human Rights Office of the High Commissioner http://www.ohchr.org [accessed 4 August 2017]

ABOUT THE AUTHOR

Barbie Latza Nadeau is an American journalist in Rome, working for *Newsweek*, *The Daily Beast* and CNN. For more than two decades she has covered crime in Europe, Italian politics, the Vatican, the refugee crisis and women's issues. Her previous book about the murder trials of Amanda Knox, *Angel Face* (2010), was adapted for film (*The Face of an Angel*, 2015), starring Kate Beckinsale as a journalist based on Barbie herself.

PRAISE FOR *ROADMAP TO HELL*

"A powerful exposé of organised crime along Italy's picturesque Amalfi Coast. *The Daily Beast's* Rome correspondent takes on gun runners, Nigerian gangs and wilfully negligent police as she chronicles the forced criminality of sex-trafficked women and drug mules – and the efforts of nuns to rescue them. Unnerving stuff."

Tatler

"Barbie Latza Nadeau dissects the intricate relationship between those who make a living from organized crime, terrorism and sex trafficking with an astute understanding of the Italian culture that allows it to prosper."

Michael Winterbottom, filmmaker

"The sex-trafficking of tens of thousands of Nigerian young women to Italy is a shamefully under-reported story that disgraces the authorities in both those countries. Barbie Latza Nadeau reveals the dirty truth with flair, forensic insight, and, above all, great empathy for the victims of this trade . . . Her tale of suffering and injustice in Italy is an uncomfortable but vital read."

Barnaby Phillips, Former BBC correspondent in Nigeria

"I read the book in one horrified gulp . . . a profound, appalling portrait of a country overwhelmed by crime, and which somehow managed to keep a focus on the human victims and the geopolitical forces at play."

Tobias Jones, author of *The Dark Heart of Italy*

"Barbie Latza Nadeau takes you on an exhilarating ride through Italy's dark underbelly."

Tina Brown

"This is a terrifying and heartbreaking book . . . I will find it difficult, from now on, to contemplate today's world without thinking about what goes on in Castel Volturno."

in Firth